ISBN 978-1-330-90167-0
PIBN 10119150

1 MONTH OF
FREE
READING

at

www.ForgottenBooks.com

By purchasing this book you are eligible for one month membership to ForgottenBooks.com, giving you unlimited access to our entire collection of over 1,000,000 titles via our web site and mobile apps.

To claim your free month visit:

www.forgottenbooks.com/free119150

English
Français
Deutsche
Italiano
Español
Português

www.forgottenbooks.com

Mythology Photography **Fiction**
Fishing Christianity **Art** Cooking
Essays Buddhism Freemasonry
Medicine **Biology** Music **Ancient
Egypt** Evolution Carpentry Physics
Dance Geology **Mathematics** Fitness
Shakespeare **Folklore** Yoga Marketing
Confidence Immortality Biographies
Poetry **Psychology** Witchcraft
Electronics Chemistry History **Law**
Accounting **Philosophy** Anthropology
Alchemy Drama Quantum Mechanics
Atheism Sexual Health **Ancient History**
Entrepreneurship Languages Sport
Paleontology Needlework Islam
Metaphysics Investment Archaeology
Parenting Statistics Criminology
Motivational

CROMWELL:

A Tragedy

IN FIVE ACTS.

BY

THE AUTHOR OF "THOMAS ABECKET," ETC.

NEW YORK:

DICK & FITZGERALD.

18 ANN STREET

C. A. ALVORD, ELECTROTYPER AND PRINTER.

TMP92-008985

OLIVER CROMWELL.

At length the world begins to understand what an honest, earnest, God-fearing man Oliver Cromwell was.

Royalist writers have dwelt much upon his low origin and the humble pursuits of his early life. He had no occasion to blush for his pedigree. His father, Robert Cromwell, having married Elizabeth Steward, purchased an establishment which had been used as a brewery.

A few years after this he died, leaving a young family to the care of their mother, who, by her skill and industry, not only provided funds to support her family in a respectable station, but even to supply her daughters with such fortunes as recommended them to suitable marriages.

This estimable lady, like Charles the First, was descended from Alexander, Lord High Steward of Scotland, and thus they were cousins in the eighth or ninth degree.

Born at Huntington, on the 25th day of April, 1599, and soon the only survivor of three sons, Oliver became a great favorite with his mother, who, though a woman of excellent sense, was of a too indulgent temper. ·

"The love of truth," says a writer of his day, "will not permit us to extol either the docility of his temper or the literary triumphs of his genius—while at school, he being described as 'playfull and obstinate.'"

Hinchinbrooke House, the seat of his uncle, Sir Oliver Cromwell, was generally one of the resting places of the royal family when on their journey from Scotland to the English capital.

In the year 1603, King James, accompanied by his young son Charles, then Duke of York, afterward King Charles the First, paid a visit to Sir Oliver Cromwell, by whom they were entertained in the most sumptuous manner.

Charles and young Oliver disagreed, and in a scuffle young Oliver drew blood from the royal nose. Sir Oliver reproved his nephew, when, it is related, King James rejoined—"Nay, nay, it will teach the boy to respect the rights of his subjects."

Milton, the immortal poet, who knew him well, does not ascribe to him high accomplishments in literature. Bishop Burnet says, "he had no foreign language, and but a little Latin."

He remained but about half the required term at the University, and was then sent to London to attend to the study of the law at Lincoln's Inn, "but making nothing of it," he soon returned home.

Sir Philip Warwick, no uncandid judge of his manhood, gives a far from flattering account of his earlier days, but says: "After a time he became converted, and declared himself ready to make restitution unto any man who would accuse him or whom he could accuse himself to have wronged. Soon thereafter he joined himself to men of his own temper who pretended unto transports and revelations."

Residing at Saint Ives, he attended the Established Church, and was intrusted with the civil business of the parish, but was not on good terms with the clergy.

Having completed his twenty-first year, he married Elizabeth, the daughter of Sir James Bouchier, of Essex, by whom he received a considerable addition to his fortune and regained the affection of his uncle, Sir Oliver, and his relations the Hampdens and Barringtons, whom he had alienated by his thoughtless or undutiful conduct.

The next seven years of his life we can learn but little of, except that he became very rigid in his manners and devoted much time to religious duties. His house was ever open to the Non-conformist ministers, whose consciences did not permit them to comply with the ritual of the Established Church. He preached in support of their principles and joined them frequently in public prayer.

This paved the way for his popularity at Huntington, and soon procured him the honor of representing that borough in the third Parliament of Charles the First. Milton says, "That being now arrived to a mature and ripe age, all which time he spent as a private person, noted for nothing so much as the culture of pure religion and an integrity of life, he was grown rich at home and had enlarged his hopes, relying upon God and a great soul in a quiet bosom for any, the most exalted times."

In his domestic life he was happy. His affection for his wife and family, being marked and tender, was by them heartily returned.

He was always active when matters of religion were brought before Parliament, and his course at an early day shows the bias which his mind had taken and the ground on which his opposition to Government was thenceforth to be maintained.

Sir Philip Warwick describes his appearance in Parliament in 1640, "as untidy in his dress, his stature of a good size, his countenance full and reddish, his voice sharp and untunable, but his eloquence full of fervor."

Discontent with Charles's administration of the Government soon leading to overt acts, we find Cromwell, at the age of 43, on the side of the people, at which period, in 1642, the play opens.

CROMWELL:

A TRAGEDY, IN FIVE ACTS.

PERSONS OF THE DRAMA.

OLIVER CROMWELL, Commoner, General, then Protector.

IRETON,
INGOLDSBY, } His sons-in-law.
FLEETWOOD,

DESBOROUGH, his brother-in-law.

PYM,
HAMPDEN, } His friends.
HOLLIS,

OLIVER and RICHARD, Cromwell's sons.

GENERAL LAMBERT, his friend.

GENTLEMEN of NORFOLK, SUFFOLK, HERTFORD, ESSEX.

WHITLOCKE, WHALLY, LENTHAL.

BRADSHAW, HARRISON, MARTIN, GRIMSHAWE, LUDLOW.

ASHE, ALLEN.

SIR HARRY VANE, COLONEL OAKEY, SIR ARTHUR HAZELRIGG.

MR. LOVE and MR. PEET, RICH, STAINES, WATSON.

MAJOR SALLOWAY, CAREW, LISLE.

LORD MAYOR OF LONDON.

AMBASSADORS from FRANCE and SPAIN.

COLONEL JEPHSON, ASHE, SIR CHARLES PACK.

ATTORNEY-GENERAL.

QUAKER FOX, a great merchant.

SPEAKER.

KING CHARLES.
REGINALD HASTINGS, } His friends.
   and others,

LADY CROMWELL, wife of Cromwell.

LADY ELIZABETH CROMWELL, his daughter.

LADY ALICE LAMBERT, wife of General Lambert.

PATIENCE, an attendant.

TRADESMEN, CITIZENS, and SOLDIERS.

Scene—ENGLAND, mostly in LONDON—A. D. 1642–1658.

CROMWELL.

ACT I.

SCENE FIRST.

A street in London.

CITIZENS *enter from opposite sides.*

FIRST CITIZEN.

Which way, my friend?

SECOND CITIZEN.

     Unto the Commons.

THIRD CITIZEN.

What for?

SECOND CITIZEN.

      To seek redress.

FIRST CITIZEN.

 To seek redress for what? The last taxes drained our
purses, robbed us and ours of our homes—why needs
our King more moneys?—we have no wars.

SECOND CITIZEN.

The Pope, who rules this wife that rules
Our King, exacts new tributes.

THIRD CITIZEN.

Down with the Pope! if needs must be,
The Queen!

FIRST CITIZEN.
And the King too!

THIRD CITIZEN.
Nay, nay, we love the King! he's Stuart blood!
Let's to the Commons!   [*Exeunt.*

SCENE SECOND.

The House of Commons.

PYM, *rising.*
Fellow-Commoners of England! her bulwark
And her boast, with love and loyalty to King Charles
I rise—if sad my visage, sorrow is at my heart—
To state that he would violate all his bonds
Demanding further supplies of us.

[HOLLIS.
And I deny that we should grant
Them to him.   At the very outset of his reign,
More a Papist than a Puritan at heart,
Charging that we, his people, sparingly doled out our
        supplies,
He, in defiance of all law, his first Parliament dissolved.
A second he convoked, but finding that
Still more intractable, its speedy dissolution
Was its fate; and he, without the show
Of legal right, fresh taxes raised, and the chiefs
Of the opposition into the cells of felons threw.
Is this the meed of patriots?

HAMPDEN.
My friends, we may not yield to these demands;
The Star-Chamber we have swept away,
The High Commission, and the Council of York.
Thomas Wentworth, late Earl of Strafford, has expiated

His great crimes by axe and block;
Laud is immured in yonder Tower;
The Lord Keeper finds refuge in a foreign land;
And King Charles has bound himself never
To adjourn, dissolve, or prorogue this Parliament,
Which here doth meet, without its own consent,
To serve its God, its country, and its King!

REGINALD HASTINGS (*Royalist*).

Ay, its wronged King!—robbed of age-founded
Hereditary rights! He loves his country.

PYM.

Indeed! then now what mean these discontents
In Ireland? The Rebellion of the Roman Catholics
In Ulster has been planned nearer home.
Our Queen one of that faith, our King of no faith
At all, though Protestant avowed.

REGINALD HASTINGS (*Royalist*).

If Church and King no reverence command,
In gentle courtesy leave our fair Queen at peace.
Heed ye well, that when the Church shall fall, then falls
        the State.

CROMWELL *enters and takes his seat on L. H., nearest foot-
lights.*

CROMWELL, *aside.*

Two fierce and eager factions it would seem,
And nearly matched. Be the King wise and true,
All will be well with him and his tried friends,
While we, perforce, must seek our homes in other climes.
But he will fail, the people's rights must triumph,
And henceforth two great parties in this realm

Shall ever contend for the mastery.

PYM.

I move that a remonstrance be presented
To the King, enumerating all the faults
Of his administration, expressing the distrust
With which his policy is still regarded
By the people, and their inability
To endure fresh taxes—but let it be expressed
In love and true allegiance.

HAMPDEN.

I second this.

CROMWELL, *aside.*

My thoughts! my sentiments! tho' gemmed in eloquence.
The current of events I'll note, and use them
As befits me.

SPEAKER.

The motion ye have heard.
All in its favor rise—

[*All rise except Royalists.*
'Tis carried—by eleven votes majority.

HOLLIS.

His Majesty promises well; but yestere'en
Falkland, Hyde, and Colepepper were invited
To become the confidential advisers
Of the Crown.

PYM.

We'll see how he will keep his promises.
But lo! whom have we here?

Enter the Attorney-General and the Sergeant-at-Arms.

SPEAKER.

What would the Attorney-General of the realm,
Of England's Commoners?

ATTORNEY-GENERAL.

Our Liege commands that I do impeach
Before the House of Lords—Lord Kimbolton,
Pym, Hollis, Hampden, Hazelrig, and Strode,
Commoners of England, for high treason.

　　Great commotion.]　Sir! sir!　[*From several voices.*

CROMWELL, *rising and advancing.*

Do I hear aright!　The King would impeach
These gentlemen?

ATTORNEY-GENERAL.

You do—the Sergeant-at-Arms,
In the King's name, demands of the House
The persons of these six gentlemen.

CROMWELL.

　　　　　　By your leave, we will consult
On this.　You may retire.　　[*Exit Attorney-General.*
　　　　　　My friends, this is too true.
* Here are private lines, just borne to me,
Which counsel that you instantly consult
Your safety.　The King himself approaches
With an armed band.

　　Great outcry.]　The King! the King!
　　　　　　　　　　　　　　[*From several voices.*

HAMPDEN.

　　　　　We'll but retire till the whirlwind's past,
And then prepare for storms—where is the treason now?

CROMWELL.

'Twere well—retire.　　　　[*Exeunt six members.*
　　Aside.]　Oh, Thou! to whom, in humble, heart-felt fealty

* From the Countess of Carlisle, sister to Northumberland.—*Hume.*
　1*

I knelt in early youth ; unto whose helping hand
I've trusting clung in manhood's stormy hours,
Nerve me with lion's strength, that singly I may brave
My country's foe, and save her from this tyranny.

    Turning to Commoners.]

Be not dismayed, my friends.   He's but a man,
Like one of us.   Now must we prove unto the wide world
For every age—that steadfast, true, God-serving hearts
Are never left to fall.   Hark! they do come.

    King CHARLES *enters with armed attendants.*

CHARLES.

Where are those whom I would impeach?

CROMWELL, advancing.

                      In safety, Sire.

CHARLES.

How so?

CROMWELL.

                    God keeps them, Sir.

CHARLES, aside.

*We battled in our youth, and he o'ermastered me,
Must we now war in our age till he o'erpowers me?

CROMWELL, advancing.

My Liege and royal kinsman, is this nobly done?
The forest's monarch, royalty's best type,
Singly pursues his prey; never in troops.

CHARLES.

Cromwell, I am—

---

    *King James paid a visit to Sir Oliver Cromwell at Hinchinbrooke
House, in September, 1604, taking with him his son Charles, when he and
the future Protector disagreed, and Oliver so little regarded the dignity
of his uncle's royal visitant, that he made the royal blood flow in copious
streams from the Prince's nose.—"*Cromwell and his Times.*"

CROMWELL.

My King, whose surest safeguard
Is his people's love, and that he best secures—

CHARLES.

Cromwell, you are our kinsman;
Else—

CROMWELL (bowing), *aside.*

The Sheriff's deputy would fulfil
His office.

My Liege, I'm, as you know,
But a plain country gentleman, not used
To courtly phrases, nor the arts that cloak
The thoughts of courtiers.   I would counsel
You in love, and beg you'd learn of nature,
And behold how the majestic monarch
Of the mount maintains his proud estate,
Spreading afar his roots in genial soil.
He on his own strength relies for vigor
To sustain his outstretched arms.

He never seeks
From arid rocks sustenance to imbibe,
Else would his branches die, his foliage fall!
The source of all your strength, your people's purse,
Is well-nigh drained—although their cup of loyalty
Still to the very brim is full.   Deem me not rude,
But banish this hired troop—'tis a rough setting,
And out of keeping with your royal heart,
Whose richest casket is your people's love.

CHARLES.

I thank you, Cromwell, for this truthfulness,
Though verily it grates ; for I have feasted
On flattery so long, that frankness

Is a new dish and out of course.   I would
That you were with me, not against me.

CROMWELL.

So am I, and would ever be, reigned you yourself,
Not food for parasites, who'd sap your strength,
Your very life, for self-advancement.

CHARLES.

I would those gentlemen would wait on us.
Counsel this, in love to us, and come with them;
We should together prop up the Stuart House,
Sprung from the self-same source—
                              I would consult with you.

CROMWELL.

Our consultation were a futile act,
Old counsellors still about you.

CHARLES.

                              But come, though
I'll not yield in this.
                    [*Exit* CHARLES *and attendants.*

CROMWELL.

There goes a noble heart, but so bewitched,
And so long trained in course of fell deceit,
That even I dare not trust him, he is
So hackneyed in these Romish ways.——
I'll see my friends and serve them if I can,
Save them I'm sure to do—
                    For this have I resolved !
Here has Charles wrecked all hopes, all chances
Of success.   Commoners of England! now assert

Your rights.   Compliance to his will ceases
To be a virtue.
　　　　　　　　Each to his home
In London; our fortress that, well garrisoned
With tried and loving hearts; urge them with prayer
True succor to entreat; and legions from the Lord
Will join our ranks.   Proclaim aloud throughout the land
Unto the wide, wide world,
"That where the Spirit of the Lord is, there is Liberty."
We are but as one man in this, I believe—
Is it not so?

　　　　　ALL *exclaim, retiring,*
　　　　　　　　　　But one! but one!

　　　　　CROMWELL, *going out.*
　　　　　　　　　　　　Let's on!

Where are the friends thou hadst,
My King, but one short hour ago?
This thy last act has made each man thy foe!　　*[Exit.*

SCENE III.

Street in London.

PYM, HAMPDEN, *and* HOLLIS, *stand on one side ; deputations from various trades pass, exclaiming,* "Privileges of Parliament! Privileges of Parliament!"

　　　　　PYM.

　　　It all works well.   The Mercers these!
And here another comes!

　　　　　HAMPDEN.

　　　The Porters these!—a God-fearing, honest
Class!   Another yet!

HOLLIS

The Apprentices! bold and reckless dare-devils
Are these, but honest as the sun.

HAMPDEN.

Stand ye apart—the King!   [*They retire one side.*
           The Beggars come
The other way—we'll note their salutation
As they meet him.
King CHARLES *enters with attendants, and they pass on.*
   Deputation of Beggars pass, exclaiming, "Privileges
   of Parliament!" *and one calls, as they pass out,* To
   your tents, O Israel!*

HAMPDEN.

       Wormwood to you, my King!
My pity for you drowns your wrongs to me.
This is Cromwell's house. We must with him consult;
Long have I known him; he is of all
" The man for the times," in spite
Of his rough exterior. If he lives, he'll be
The foremost man of every age.   [*Exeunt.*

SCENE FOURTH.

Interior of Cromwell's House.

CROMWELL, *alone, strides across the stage.*
This fire at my heart o'erheats my brain!
Would I could play the woman, and in tears
Weep out my rage—no! no! they would but scald

---

* The words employed by the mutinous Israelites when they abandoned
Rehoboam, their rash and ill-counselled sovereign.—*Hume.*—*Clarendon.*

My furrowed cheeks, and sear with life-long scars.

    *   *   *   *   *

To think that men so gentle and so pure,
So elevate in nature, that they look
On earthly pride and pomp, as shines the sun
Upon this tinselled scene, mere work of men's weak hands,
Should be thus hunted down like wolves,
While, lamb-like, spite of all their wrongs,
They are bleating out their love for him,
And urging gentle treatment of their tyrant King.

LADY CROMWELL enters.

My Lord, my loving Lord! what moves you thus?

CROMWELL.

My dearest wife, thy love ever was the brook
Whereat I slaked my thirst and cooled
My fevered brow.   By nature I was never gentle:
Rough and uncouth in form, unhammered iron
Both my heart and hand—I am o'erwrought to-day;
But now thou comest, I shall grow calm and cool,
For you can mould me as you will, dear love.

LADY CROMWELL.

But what is this, my Lord?

CROMWELL.

Hast thou not heard, how, mid the hot debate
Upon his new demands,—Pym, Hampden,
Hollis, and our friends, urging a mild remonstrance
To his will and wishes,—first there comes
A message from the King, that they should be impeached,
And then a secret letter sent to me,
Informing that in person he would seek them,
Of which I instantly advised.

Scarce had the Attorney left the Commons, when the
    King,
Forgetful of all promises, all pledges,
Forgetful of his honor as a man,
Forgetful of the sacred office of a king,
And all its great attendants, rushed in
With a rude band of hired menials,
And did demand the persons of these gentlemen!

LADY CROMWELL.

You did not yield them up?

CROMWELL.

                        No, but I told him
That God kept them, as He ever does the just;
That He would preserve them.

LADY CROMWELL.

        Spake you thus unto the King, my Lord?

CROMWELL.

I did; in what is he more than mortal like us?

LADY CROMWELL.

His power!

CROMWELL.

        He has no power now.   He had
Until this hour; till now the Commons inclined
To him, despite of all their wrongs.
But this last act awoke the slumbering fires
At their hearts; the ebullitions of their rage
Burst forth as the long smothered volcano's flames,
And swallowed all things up.   The streets of London
Are with hot lava filled; none but spirits kindred
To them may safely sojourn there.
     Enter PYM, HAMPDEN, *and* HOLLIS.
Gentlemen, you're welcome, very welcome!   Here

For a time you're safe !   [*Shouts heard.*]

                    What means this outcry
And this violence ?

PYM.

          Our wrongs have taken voice :
All London is aroused.

HAMPDEN.

                         And we must seek
How best to quell this turbulence.

CROMWELL.

                    True, true !
It were not well that it should spend itself;
We yet may need some little fire to light
Us on our way.   Hampden, we have too tamely borne
Our wrongs, more like weak children, 'neath the brutal
          rule
Of some tyrant guardian, than the people's friends,
Intrusted with the care of their dearest rights.
Strike not these shouts with leaden weight upon your
          hearts,
Upbraiding as they fall ?

HOLLIS.

                    They do ; and we must act
For them, if Charles dissolves not our Parliament.

CROMWELL, *much excited.*

Dissolve this Parliament !   He shall tear
· This form limb from limb,
Till that the weak pulsation of this heart
Shall be sole sign that ever it was mortal,
Ere he shall dare do that !   We have been too tame !
          *   *   *   *   *   *

I have advised that Parliament seize the town of Hull,

Where there is now a magazine of arms;
That Goring, at Portsmouth, be required
To obey no commands but theirs;
And instant arming of the Londoners
Take place.   That Essex be made General
Of Parliament—but here is Ireton!
   IRETON *enters.*]   What news, my son?

IRETON.

The people all enraged, the King has gone
To York, whither the nobility, in crowds,
Do follow him.

CROMWELL.

              Nobility!
The tinselled nobles follow him.   He
Is their only hope.   I would he had them all;
Their touch but taints;
The true nobility are ours!   What more?

IRETON.

Essex is made General of the Parliamentary forces,
And news is just received that Charles has raised
His standard at Nottingham.

CROMWELL.

'Tis well! England is born again!
After a slumber of six hundred years,*
The Anglo-Saxon shall awake to life!
Where was thy guardian angel, treacherous King,†
When thou compelledst that small band
Of peaceful spirits who had embarked
For the new world to disembark, and, toiling, here,
Drag out a mean existence, when plenty,
Peace, virtue, Religion, there were free,
As God first made them unto all mankind?
Since thou wouldst have me great, thou must not murmur

---

   * A'Becket's murder.   † 1634.

That thou madest me so.　Though I may never tread
New England's virgin soil—bear through her wondrous
　　　wilds
The banner of the Lord—teach the Red Man
That his Great Spirit is ours—that we are but one—
I'll sow such seeds that ages yet unborn,
Throughout the world, shall bless the day
Cromwell from peaceful intents was torn,
And forced to be a Man.
　　　　　　　　But much there is to do;
King Charles's army will be in bright plumage decked;
Rupert is a master-spirit in the charge,—
He has trained troops, while we have, at best,
A rabble crew, will never stand the onset
Of the foe!
　　　　　　Gentlemen, do you each to your
Several homes.　Hollis, in London, enroll
The stoutest artisans of our faith.
Pym, there are many kindred spirits will follow
You where fiercest is the fight; drill them
Into strict obedience, for a steady front
Is what we most shall need.　Hampden, my friend,
At your own home there are at least a thousand
True and steadfast hearts; hasten you thither,
And prepare them all, and let each and every man
Account himself the Lord's.　Ireton will to his friends,
And raise a troop of horse; while I'll　　Ely,
And arouse all mine.　　*　　　*　　　*to
　　　　　　　Pardon me, gentlemen,
In counselling thus the choicest spirits
Of the land,—myself an humble citizen,
Though servitor of God,—I do presume too much.

HAMPDEN.

We came not, Cromwell, for honeyed words,

But counsel, and you counsel give,—such counsel
As we sought.   The whirlwind bows all trees
Of weaker growth ; old England's oak still holds
His head erect, an emblem for us all.
Be thou that oak !

CROMWELL.

Then since you've sought from me, let us,
Each and all, distrustful of his single strength,
Seek from our God His guidance and support;
And with a pledge, that, as we shall strive
But for our England's honor and supremacy,
So when her *people's rights* are well secured,
We'll lay aside our arms.

[*Exeunt* PYM, HAMPDEN, *and* HOLLIS.
Enter, on opposite side, his daughter ELIZABETH, *son*
OLIVER, *and* LADY LAMBERT.

My own fair daughter and my gallant son ;
And thou ! most lovely Lady Lambert, dost thou brave
This   scene,   venturing through London's   waves tem-
        pestuous,
To see how fiercely they are chafing here?

[*Striking his breast.*

My children dear, ever does kind Heaven send
Its comforts with its cares.

LADY LAMBERT.

                My husband absent,
It were but fitting that his glory's partner
Should learn what griefs assail our cause,
That she might timely forewarn him in words
Of gentlest love, not let them rudely burst
Upon his ear, too oft assailed already ;
Emboldened by these thoughts, your most fair daughter,
Venus-like, ushered me to the light of day,
Thou England's Sun !

CROMWELL.

Grace in your speech, no less
Than in your form!—henceforth shall Cromwell
E'er in heaviest hours welcome you,
Dearest lady, amidst these his best counsellors
(As such, my wife and children ever proudly owned).
My son, it seems the will and pleasure
Of the Lord that I, who his servitor
So long have been, should take an active,
It may be, foremost part with my long well-tried friends
In England's cause.

OLIVER.

Father, the King!

CROMWELL.

Reigns, son, but for himself.
He doth forget the trust God hath reposed in him,
Thus choosing him His Vicegerent.   Go you with Ireton,
Your brother now—a father in my absence he will be
To you.   Ireton! my eldest son,—the hope and love
Of manhood's earliest hours, the pride of present years,
And promise of my age,—I do intrust to you;
Make him a soldier, but a soldier in the Lord;
A warrior like yourself, I ask no more;
Now take him with you, and enroll your horse.

IRETON.

Father, it shall be so.

OLIVER.

Come, Ireton, I am eager
For the fight; I'll not disgrace my lineage
Or my name.

CROMWELL.

Well said, my son, may Heaven be with you.

IRETON.

Hark! "Cromwell" fills the air as well as gilds the walls;
All London's streets proclaim the people's will,
And call to arms.   [*Exeunt* IRETON *and young* OLIVER.

CROMWELL.

Not theirs, but God's!
His high behest I must, I will obey.   [*Exit* CROMWELL.

LADY ELIZABETH.

O dearest Lady! what a rived heart is mine;
My duty weighed against my love.   I may not pray
For either cause.

LADY LAMBERT.

Cheer thee, dear girl!   Your father
Is no foe unto the King, but unto his dishonor.

LADY ELIZABETH.

Think you that he will hearken to our love?

LADY LAMBERT.

You are as nobly born as this Young Charles,
But custom sanctions not an honorable love
Between the prince and subject.

LADY ELIZABETH.

Sweet friend,
That is the worm that gnaws!   No other
Ever could be mine,—none other would Charles have;
He loves me purely, worships me as though
I were a saint from Heaven.

LADY LAMBERT.

I pray thee, think no more of it,
Insatiate—it is man's way—but satisfied—beware!
He is by birth a King!   They deem all creatures
Made but for their pleasure and their will—ay,

Even earth's fairest, such as thou, sweet girl.
Beware! beware!   [*Exeunt.*

SCENE FIFTH.

A Large Tent.—An Encampment.—Night—Table, Books, and Taper.

CROMWELL.

Is this a dream, or dread reality?
Have those strange thoughts I dwelt on in my youth
Thus taken form and shape? or have I on visions
So long feasted that my mind, o'erwrought, wanders
Mid quicksands will my hopes ingulf?
'Tis night; no sound, save the trusty sentinel's tread,
Who keeps his watch, humming some holy strain,
And praying God to guard his earthly hopes
As he shall guard His cause.
                              It is no dream.
A nation's wrongs have forced a nation's heart
To burst the cerements of kingly love,
And make a bold assertion of their rights;
Rights born of Heaven, conferred by God;
Not to be lightly or unvalued worn.
    Kneeling.]   His hand I see in this—to whom I kneel
In humble supplication for His aid,
His counsel, and His care.   A distant tread—
A challenge—they have passed;
It is those valued friends I summoned here.
I summoned here!—Why would they make me first?
Essex and Fairfax are of nobler rank,
Though not more *nobly born.*   For am not I
A kinsman of the King?—might have been
King myself! might have been king myself?
I see no weird women on this heath;

There are no spirits in the air, I know,
To whisper this to me! It is no whisper,
Though it sounds as though 'twere thunder-born,
And drowns my every thought but this:
That I might have been king! And so I might,
As well as he who now doth wear the diadem:
From Alexander, Lord High Steward of Scotland,*
Both are sprung—Charles traces back through a long
    line of kings,
His ancestor being the elder son; while I
Am scion of that noble house, descended
Through my sainted mother, eleventh in succession
From that Lord's third son, while Charles is but the
    twelfth
From his eldest born.
There glares the curse of primogeniture!
The times have changed, and so must human courses.
I will be king—king in the service of the King of kings,
And reign pre-eminent o'er the hearts of men.
[*Enter several gentlemen escorted by the sentinel.*]
My friends.

GENTLEMAN.

            Cromwell, your messenger urged
All haste, or we had not intruded on the night
With the day's business.

CROMWELL.

            You're very welcome,
And I thank you heartily. So long unused
To every public charge,—my little knowledge
Being but from books,—this glittering harness
But uneasily fits, and, like an untutored steed,
I must be trained to it. But now I learn
That Lord Capel advances upon Cambridge

---

              * Noble.

With both horse and foot; that many
Of the old nobility are hastening up in arms.
  Aside.] I'll sound these gentlemen!—
"We must consider seriously, my friends, how acceptable
" A service to the King ours would be,
" To keep five whole counties in his obedience."

GENTLEMAN.

Is there then hope of him?

CROMWELL.

There is always hope with life. Bad counsellors
Are his curse. We must be a sheet-anchor
To the State; fast holding amid the gales
That fiercely assail her now; but see
What honors, what rewards, the storm o'erpast,
We then may justly claim for such true loyalty.
" What troops are there in Essex now, who have
" The honor and happiness of the King at heart?"

GENTLEMAN OF ESSEX.

Three thousand; two of stalwart hearts on foot,
One thousand the best mounted in the land.

CROMWELL.

I know your stables are most choicely filled;
Your riders are?

GENTLEMAN OF SUSSEX.

A God-fearing, prayerful, preachful set—

CROMWELL.

In our cause chief elements of success.
And yours of Suffolk?

GENTLEMAN OF SUFFOLK.

Two thousand—all well-armed, brave artisans.

CROMWELL.

A brawny race—I've met with them.   And yours
Of Hertford?

GENTLEMAN OF HERTFORD.

Three thousand and three hundred
When all told—with most delicious voices
And great prayers.

CROMWELL, *smiling.*

Less music shall we need, then.
'Tis very well—for 'tis expensive, and all we save
We gain.   And how of Norfolk?

GENTLEMAN OF NORFOLK.

Jockeys in Norfolk,—
Every man's a horse.   Some fifteen hundred
Chanting cherubs, with good steeds,
And fifteen hundred well mounted as at their birth.

CROMWELL.

You're pleasant, sir!

GENTLEMAN OF NORFOLK.

It is but pleasure that I've entered on—
A game of chance—'tis true, a boisterous game.
The winner—who can tell?

CROMWELL, *aside.*

'Tis a shrewd fellow—what does he mean?
Ironically.]   Gentlemen, you deserve
Much love and many honors from your King.
Meet me here with your best speed, six days
From this, with all the forces you can raise.
Bring all your saints from Hertford, and Norfolk's
Chanting cherubs!   [*Exeunt Gentlemen.*
A saintly crew—I'll use them.

Sentinel enters and hands papers.]
What now ? from London ! from Hampden, too ?
Reads.] "Spare nor goad nor spur, but speed to London ;
Now the Commons sit in consultation
Upon proposals made by the Lords in favor
Of a peace.   Haste, or our cause is lost——"
Lost ! Lost ! no, no ! thou noble spirit, tried friend,
And truest gentleman that England boasts.
No cause is lost, with Hampden on its side.
God watches with the virtuous—they ne'er fail ;
Though they may fall, 'tis but as sets the sun to-day
To rise the brighter on to-morrow's morn.
True virtue never fails——
                My horse—my fleetest horse !
My Ironsides, an' you will——
    GENERAL LAMBERT *enters.*] Remain you in command,
My trusty friend, for I must post to London.
Read this—it is for thee alone ; observe
The strictest discipline—religious exercises
Thrice a day ; with purest sentiments inspire
The men ; let them have no time for idle thoughts
Or ribald jests.
And this, the " Soldier's Bible,"* give to each,
Where, from the Holy Scriptures,—THE CHARTERS
OF THE LIBERTIES OF MANKIND,—selections
Most appropriate may be found ;
Thus may each daily say or sing
The praises of his God.
              The morn now breaks,
And I must speed away on matters of great moment

---

* Cromwell had appropriate quotations made from the Holy Scriptures,
printed upon a sheet folded into sixteen pages, a copy of which was given
to every soldier under his command.

To our cause—   [*Distant Reveillé heard.*
" What is to do?   I know not what I would have,
Though I know what I would not have."

GENERAL LAMBERT.

You have not rested now for some three nights;
Nature will be outworn—

CROMWELL.

                    Good friend, my country calls;
I may nòt rest for many a night—
    Aside.]   It may be never more.
Farewell! God speed you all.

LAMBERT *walks back towards the tent.* CROMWELL *exits.*

Curtain falls slowly.

END OF ACT I.

ACT II.

SCENE FIRST.

Room in Cromwell's House.

LADY CROMWELL, LADY ALICE LAMBERT, *and* LADY
ELIZABETH CROMWELL, *enter.*

LADY CROMWELL.

Hark, how the shouts of a maddened populace
Come like the surges of a raging sea,
Lashed into fury by contending winds,
Proclaiming some new-born wrongs heaped
On their already overloaded backs!   My King,
My King, why goad them unto frenzy?

LADY LAMBERT.

The roar hath passed,
And now falls on the ear as murmur
Of a distant sea, subsiding into peace.

LADY ELIZABETH.

Yes, lady mother, now notes of joy and voices
Of glad welcome fill the air, as though
Some mighty conqueror approached, laden
With new-born honors.

LADY CROMWELL.

'Tis Pym they name, and Hampden,
Cromwell's friends.   Why do they rank him first?
Would we were safe upon New England's shore!
I dread this sudden greatness.   My King! my King!
Oh, thou art ill-advised; thy gentle, true,

And trusting nature is abused.   Why cast
You from you all would be your friends,
And leap into this den?   Sweet Lady Alice,
Where is now your lord?   Lambert has potent voice
With this rude crowd.   He should be here
When Cromwell is away.

LADY LAMBERT.

It is thy Lord Cromwell's order he observes,
That keeps him from the hearts that love him best.
The Parliament sent him hence to raise
Fresh troops, and he returns not till they summon him.
But here are worthy gentlemen—
                    Hampden, England's pearl,
And Pym, the gorgeous ruby of the times.

HAMPDEN *and* PYM *enter, saying,*

                    At your service, ladies.

LADY CROMWELL.

You're very welcome, gentlemen, for our woman fears
Have magnified the noise in London's streets
Into things terrible, and our timid hearts
Beat quickly for those friends we know do brave
The storms.   When hast thou heard from my honored
        Lord?—
'Tis strange that I must question you of him,—
I, who ne'er passed a day without his smiles,
From that proud hour when first I called him
Lord, till, leaving Nature's bright and lovely walks,
We sought a home mid London's dreary walls.

HAMPDEN.

You may expect him ere the sun hath set;
Most urgent matters call him here.   [*Giving letters.*

Sweet Lady Lambert, from your honored Lord,
A trusty messenger these lines hath brought.

LADY ALICE,

My Lord! my honored Lord!—

HAMPDEN.

Most fair Elizabeth, thy smiles I woo
To win me to forgetfulness.   Would that I had
A son, and he might win your love, that I might call
You daughter—thou brightest jewel in our Cromwell's
  home.

LADY ELIZABETH.

Kind Sir, I am not worthy of such praise,
Far, far more honored than my poor deserts,
By your o'er-estimate—
       [CROMWELL *enters.*
Rushes to CROMWELL.]   My father, my dear father!

CROMWELL *salutes each.*

My child, my dearest child, my honored wife,
Fair Lady Alice,—and my friends—
    [*Giving a hand to* HAMPDEN *and* PYM.
    My friends, ye are true friends
Indeed,—thus, mid the many calls our country
Makes, to offer solace to these o'ertasked hearts.
Hampden, how idle are the glories of the world;
How vain, illusory, the gifts which shine
Most gorgeous to our view!   How rich in blessings
Is that peaceful country life, where we had dwelt
So long.   How valued was the privilege granted us
Of studying in great Nature's book,
Written by God's own hand.   I am already
Sickening of this scene of turmoil and of strife,
And envy even the untutored savage

Who may roam at will, and worship the Great Spirit
Unrestrained, in Nature's wondrous temples—
His, his is freedom—there the soul may soar
Where'er its Godlike nature bears it,
And such adoration render as the spirit
Feels, of essence like itself.

      'Tis not the material form
That alone untrammelled makes us freemen ;
But the immaterial sense that teaches us
That we are heavenly born—that this life's
But a pilgrimage.

LADY CROMWELL.

      My dearest Lord, you think
Too deeply ; you magnify our cares !
God gives us charges, but He gives us, too,
Ability to fulfil them ; he praises best,
And the best service renders, who loveth best
Whatever is imposed by Him. There is
Some occult blessing e'er in store, whatever our trials.

CROMWELL.

True, my sweet comforter—my saint-like wife—
Seeing letter in LADY ALICE's *hand, who starts.*]
Fair Lady Alice ! From your lord, I ween—
      How fares my friend ?

LADY ALICE.

Well as his friends could wish.

CROMWELL.

Shouts heard.] Hampden, what mean these cheers ?

HAMPDEN, *going to window.*

Cheers for our friends—our true and steadfast friends.
Unto the Lords' proposal for a peace,

The Commons had well-nigh yielded;
For two long nights, an angry, hot debate
Gave us but a slight majority.

CROMWELL.

What! are we, then, so weak in friends,
Or were they overawed?

PYM.

Uncertain of their strength;
And hearing Charles gathered fresh forces
Every hour, many did quiver, while
Some men quailed!

CROMWELL.

Brave hearts! Why, they should tougher grow,
Like steel, the more they are hammered on.
This gives *me* new strength! What said the Londoners
To this?

HAMPDEN.

They called them cowards, truants
To the trust the people had reposed in them.
Now, the foremost of our citizens do parade
The streets with drums, and fifes, and martial music;
While banners flaunt the air; and call
Upon the populace to enroll in the defence of London.

CROMWELL.

This, that daunts them, gives me new strength,
Nerves me for mightier trials. I'll seek
Their leaders, and inflame their hearts
With the pure fires of Liberty!
This is no time
For woman's fears! Quivered and quailed,
You said, when that their country's welfare
2*

Was at stake—   [*Turning to his daughter.*
        Why, I would offer up this,
My dearest child, on Liberty's altar,
For a sacrifice, and deem it cheaply bought,
Though my heart writhed in agony at the deed!
Come, we'll unto our friends.
Exeunt Ladies on one side.]
        [CROMWELL, PYM, *and* HAMPDEN *exeunt on the other.*

SCENE SECOND.

Streets of London, at nightfall.—Popular Commotion.

FIRST CITIZEN.

Down with these fickle Commoners, and give us men!

SECOND CITIZEN.

Give us those spirits dare assert our rights!

THIRD CITIZEN.

Men sprung from Nature; not the tinselled forms
That glisten, to dim at the mere touch of breath.

FOURTH CITIZEN.

Give us our Pym!

FIFTH CITIZEN.

        Our Hampden!

SIXTH CITIZEN.

                Our Hollis!   But here they come.
Enter PYM, HAMPDEN, *and* HOLLIS.

HOLLIS.

Thanks, my friends, thanks; this gives me hope;
For I had feared Peace had most truly rusted out

Not only our arms, but hearts ; that our English valor,
So famed, was gone.
But twenty miles apart, for ten days the foes sought each
      other.
The battle of Edgehill was fought; and he who was
The conqueror, after a good night's repose,
First left the field!   Essex retiring to Warwick
With his carpet knights ;
The King, with his show troops, too glad to escape
A second fight, fell back on his old post
At Banbury, leaving five thousand Englishmen
On the field.   This Rupert is a hot-headed
And bold partisan—unequalled
In the sudden and fierce onslaught ;—
But there's, as yet, no general in the field.

HAMPDEN.

But there is in the LAND.   The man is born
That shall be styled—
           "THE BEST THING EVER ENGLAND DID."
Nurtured in peaceful arts, of stalwart form,
Sustained in all his trials by his faith in God ;
Looking on life, as written in His book,
A scene of obligations must be filled
By each in his due course ; not seeking
How he may evade, to him, God's seeming stern,
But justice-born commands.

CITIZENS.

Cheers for Hampden, Hollis, Pym—
Cromwell enters.]   And Cromwell, too.
Cheers for the people's friends.

HAMPDEN.

Thanks, thanks, my gentle friends.

CROMWELL.

Thanks, thanks, ye noble hearts, no longer
Would be slaves. 'Tis true, in loyalty you love
Your King; but he's no King who violates
All rights, all obligations, and forgets his royalty.
For royalty is born of God, and to be honored,
Must be worn as wears the Lord his attributes.
Has not he raised his banner against you
At Northampton? Has not Edgehill been fought,
And Marston Moor? The reeking wounds of thousands
    call from earth
For vengeance on their heads so ill advise,
While hosts of departed spirits knock
At Heaven's gate, witnesses from this dread scene;
I would not stir you up to rage by asking
Of those dearest friends you've lost; I would not wake
The sleeping lion at your hearts by asking
For your butchered young!
                But, in Religion's name,
I'd ask if 'tis ordained, expressed,
Or even implied, that one man's wicked will
Shall trample on a nation's rights? I find
No record of it in the Word of God,—
The true authority for all man's acts.
Some are there, who would have you yield tamely,
Submissively; I tell you, no! You have a sacred trust,
Untarnished to transmit to ages yet unborn.
But let your work be in the spirit of the Lord!
Consider deeply, how high the trust that God
Has given in endowing reason—likening
To himself mere worms of earth. See how the world
Has grown in temporal, since spiritual gifts
To it were known! The seed is sown, the culture

By Heaven taught, the harvest's all your own.
Your King has forced you into arms ;
For years you've tamely borne all your wrongs
Granting supplies—for what ? that while you're poor
He and his pampered menials might be rich.
There is no halo hanging about his name ;
Has England's glory ever been his aim ?
Is there one single act, in all his long and peaceful reign,
Adorns the page of history ? No !
But his wilful violations of your rights
Outnumber the sea-shore's sands !
I would not urge you, friends, against your King ;
There's a divinity doth guard that name.
But since this Charles has raised his standard
Against his people and their Heaven-born rights,
He has become no more than their common foe.
When he is mindful of his proud estate,
Transmitted to him through a line of kings,
Banishes from his side the assassins of England's honor,
He will be in his people's hearts enthroned,
And there more proudly gemmed than e'er was
Egypt's queen ; religions hosts his never-sleeping guard,
So long as virtue shines his diadem.
In the mean time, prepare we for the worst ;
Forewarned, hereafter we must be found forearmed.
I must to the field and face this " people's foe." [*Exeunt.*

SCENE THIRD.

Room in Cromwell's House—Morning.

LADY CROMWELL, LADY LAMBERT, *and* LADY ELIZABETH
at a table, sewing. PATIENCE, *an attendant.*

LADY CROMWELL.

Good Patience, thou hast brought no news to-day.
Go hearken what the gossips say below.
[*Exit* PATIENCE.
Dear Lady Alice and my fair daughter,
The one the bride of Lambert—you our Cromwell's pride,
There is sad news to-day! Charles and his friends
Are carrying all before them in the west.
At Stratton they have overcome our Stamford;
At Lawnsdown, too, with dreadful loss of life,
The Royalists gained the victory; and Bristol,
Second city in the land, in riches and in greatness,
Has been taken.

LADY ALICE.

My Lord—

LADY CROMWELL.

Is safe with Essex—[*to Elizabeth*] where your father is.

LADY ELIZABETH, *aside.*

My father! mine's a divided interest.
Which father do I mean—my source and spring of life,
Or him, my source of hope, love, happiness,—
The father of my Charles? Oh, dreadful day
That ever I was born to know such misery!

LADY CROMWELL.

Who comes?
Pym *and* Hampden *enter.*]

PYM.

Your friends and servitors.

LADY CROMWELL.

What news?

PYM.

None but ill news.
A king is warring against his people;
His people, serpent-like, against themselves.
Our Edmund Waller—the courtly gentleman,
The poet, scholar, and the soul, 'twas thought,
Of honor—has been detected in a foul conspiracy.
He and his brother Tompkins and friend Chaloner
Are hung!   There was no course but this.

HAMPDEN.

The battle of Newbury has been fought
And the pure Falkland's fallen, with "peace"
Upon his lips.   Both armies worsted—London's militia,
As Anglo-Saxons ever do, equalling the veteran's valor—
Have retired to winter quarters, and we may soon
Expect our friends.   Essex is no great general.

LADY ALICE.

Then Cromwell will be home—your Lord and my Lord—
Lambert will be home!

LADY ELIZABETH, *aside.*

And my Charles, where?

PYM.

Your Cromwell is the soul of our arms.
He found a rabble crew, and formed
A bulwark for our liberties.
              In Newbury's fight
Our troops were felled by Rupert's fierce onslaught
As hurricane fells forest-trees, till Cromwell
With his netted foot, his mettled cavalry,
A rocky front opposed, as breasts the firm-based mount,.
Now frowning in the clouds, now in the sunshine gleaming,
The waves that lash its iron sides—mere mockery.
Fairfax and CROMWELL are our sole hope,
His name alone a legion.
              Yet more than this,
He's not found only in the fiercest fight,
But in the Council stands pre-eminent;
Let but a friend of Cromwell's propose a step,
And all the way shines bright, where was but gloom.
Were he like us, seeing no Charles, all would be well.
His kinsman of England, with his regal rights,
Falls like a shadow on his noble heart
And palls his arm—though all his *love* is England's.

HAMPDEN.

We have one hope, and that is, that this Charles
May yet be guilty of deceit towards him,
And sever all their bonds. My friend—
   IRETON *enters.*]

IRETON.

Is my friend Cromwell here?—my father,
For I have won that name winning his daughter's love.

   CROMWELL *enters.*]

PYM.

My country's hope!

IRETON.

My father!

LADY CROMWELL.

My honored lord!

LADY ELIZABETH.

My father!

LADY ALICE.

And my—friend!

CROMWELL.

Love and esteem to each and all—
                         My honorable wife!
    To LADY ALICE.]   My lovely lady! my children!
    To PYM.]   Mine and England's truest friend,
You've seen the cloud that lowers in our skies
Coming as comes the snow, a leaden pall,
Sent from the Ice-King's Court, as though in league
Against us.   You'll see it all dispelled
As morning mist before the Day-King's messenger.
Ray after ray now rises, and each one glistens
Brighter than the last; rolling its folds away.
I would preserve my King, while quelling
Our foes; I would that he might wear his royalty—
An emanation from the Deity;
If he will not, he is no King.   He summons now
One portion of the land to war upon the other.
Scotland is all in arms, and in his cause
Would wreak her vengeance upon England
For her imagined wrongs—wrongs which have made
Her great.   One of the brightest jewels

In earth's diadem, "*Great* Britain" speaks
Her fame unto the wide, wide world.

IRETON.

You, her general, speak of others' wrongs;
Sees thy noble nature not thy own?

CROMWELL.

What means my son? thy brow is clouded.

IRETON.

Thine ear apart—these women and their tongues!—

CROMWELL.

Indeed—it must be weighty.
  CROMWELL *and* IRETON *apart*.] [*Exeunt others.*

IRETON.

Since you took Hilsdon House and kept Oxford
In alarm, even the foe do pit you against
Prince Rupert; the King, hearing this, himself
Exclaimed:
 "I would some one would do me
The good service to bring Cromwell to me,
Alive or dead."

CROMWELL.

    He flatters me!
But I'll not favor him with my presence yet.
The time will come when we'll stand front to front.

IRETON.

But more, he has dispatched letters to the Queen
Touching your life.

CROMWELL.

    My life! 'tis in God's hands!

IRETON.

Concealed in a saddle—-they will be sent
To a certain tavern on the coast near this,
And thence to France.

CROMWELL.

We will dispatch some trusty friends
To seize them—yet stay, we'll be those friends
Ourselves.   Come, you are ever ready
For the scene of danger.   We'll seize this saddle
Ourselves.   It may not prove an easy one
To Charles.   We'll borrow some troopers' cloaks
And morions.   Come, away!   [*Exeunt.*

SCENE FOURTH.

A Camp.—Parliamentary Officers advance.—General's tent in front.

FIRST OFFICER.

So a deputation has been sent to Scotland
To negotiate a treaty.
                     Our lamb-like Parliament
Are sick of war, ere they have heard its sound.
Our troops too, all unpaid, as well as we—
Where is our General Cromwell?   He is the man
For times like these!   Essex and Fairfax
Are too tamely given.

SECOND OFFICER.

                     Too true, alas!—for now the battle
Of Naseby is fought, and Colonel Monk has joined
Our cause—but here comes Ireton, and Cromwell too.
     IRETON *and* CROMWELL *enter.*]

CROMWELL, *with a letter.*

Weak and perfidious tyrant! Here has he sealed
His own destruction.
                        Forsooth he is courted
Alike by both factions, but rather thinks
To close with the Presbyterians.
                        His French Madam,
Her whom they ycleped our Queen, reproaches
Him with making too large concessions
To those villains;—and here he writes:
" But, dear heart, rest thou assured
That I shall in due time know what to do
With these rogues, who, instead of a silken leash,
Shall be fitted with a hempen cord."
Look to it, Charles, thy head is not so firm
On thy shoulders as it was an hour since.

IRETON.

It may be he thus speaks to please his dame.

CROMWELL.

And so would hang us some fair day,
By way of gallantry to his spouse!
There is no longer a King in England!
Her monarchy died within the hour,
Though it be aged sixteen hundred years.
Harrison, return at once to camp! Arouse
Our troops! rekindle the stifled flames
Into a blaze!—restore the confidence
Of the army in its leaders; assure them
We have abandoned all intention
In favor of this King.
                        Ireton, what said

The Parliament to the conditions I would propose
Unto the King ?

IRETON.

They did address them to him,
And he returned an obstinate refusal.

CROMWELL.

What then ?   Speak quickly !

IRETON.

The vote of non-addresses was passed.

CROMWELL.

Then is Charles in fact, though not in words,
Dethroned !
   We will keep down by military awe
The majority in Parliament.

IRETON.

   But blow after blow on all sides falls upon us!
The Scots invade !   The fleets in the Thames
Have hoisted the royal colors ; risings
In Norfolk, Suffolk, Essex, Kent, and Wales ;
Divisions among ourselves—Fairfax,
Governed either by his wife or by his rigid
Presbyterian principles, refused to lead
Against the Scots.   May it not be suspected
That these movements are contemplated
With secret complacency by a majority
Of the Lords and Commons ?

CROMWELL.

    What of that ?
He is not the only general in the land—
We'll find another.   The Master Genius
Of the times shall rise, and against all

Alone suffice;—who greater, purer, than our Hampden?
Hasten you unto Fairfax; govern him;
See that he suppress the insurrection
In the South. In Wales I will subdue the revolt;
And while they think me there, I will to Scotland.
I'll drive them to their hills—these Highland Chiefs.
Haste ye to the South! keep up the drooping spirits
Of our troops.

IRETON.

It shall be done. Fare you well.
Giving letter.] But ha! I did forget—I found this letter
In my tent—it is addressed unto the troops.

CROMWELL.

Ha! Ha-a-a-a! What devil's work is this? Ho, there!
Soldier enters.]
Are my brave fellows prepared for the review?
We soon shall meet the foe.
The victory must be ours.

SOLDIER.

They but await their General.

CROMWELL.

I will attend.
[*Exeunt* CROMWELL *and others through his tent.*

SCENE FIFTH.

Scene changes to troops drawn up in line prepared for the Review—Let
this be done by drawing aside the General's Tent.

CROMWELL *advances with Officers—a letter in his hand—
and says:*

Ha! My brave soldiers in the Lord—
What! Discontent? What! Fears? Whose lines

Are these would stir you to revolt?

                              To revolt
Against whom?   Against yourselves—for 'tis yourselves
Who would fall, if you fail.   Has not
" The Almighty set his Canon against
Self-slaughter?"   'Tis this it bids you do—
A suicidal act—No! no! it cannot be—
The bare thought of such a dreadful deed
Strikes terror in your hearts, and tears, I see—
Tears of contrition, the only tears
The Independent soldier ever sheds,—
Steal mournfully down your cheeks.

                              I can no more—
You never will, I know, desert your Lord!
Desert your wives—your babes—your homes!
Desert your General and this holy cause!

                    TROOPS.

Never! never! never!
Rear high our standard—lead us to the fight!

          CROMWELL, *unfurling a flag.*

The victory is won!—" The Lord of Hosts is with us!
The God of Jacob is our refuge."—On, Ironsides, on!

                    TABLEAU.

          Curtain Falls.

ACT III.

SCENE FIRST.

Streets of London—Whitehall.

A crowd of Citizens.

FIRST CITIZEN.

The King! the King!

SECOND CITIZEN.

What king?

THIRD CITIZEN.

Why our King, King Charles,
Escorted now from Hurst to Windsor
By our Colonel Harrison.

FOURTH CITIZEN.

What, have we earthed the fox at last,
Despite of all his cunning ? "He who publicly recognized*
The houses at Westminster as a legal Parliament,
And at the same time made a private minute
In Council declaring the recognition null.

FIFTH CITIZEN.

Ay, and publicly disclaimed all thought
Of calling in foreign aid against his people;
At the same time privately soliciting it
From France, Denmark, and Lorraine.

SIXTH CITIZEN.

He denied that he employed Papists, at the same time
Privately sent to his generals, directions to employ

* Macaulay

Every Papist that would serve ; publicly
Took the Sacrament at Oxford, as a pledge
That he never would even connive at Popery ;
Privately assured his Popish wife that he intended
To tolerate it in England, and authorized
Lord Glamorgan to promise that it should
Be established in Ireland—and then attempted
To clear himself at his agent's expense,
Who received, in the royal handwriting,
Reprimands, intended to be read by others,
And eulogies, to be seen but by himself.
Why, even his most devoted friends complain
Among themselves, with bitter grief and shame,
Of his crooked politics.　His defeats, they say,
Give them less pain than his intrigues."

SEVENTH CITIZEN.

A prisoner, he will seek to cajole
And undermine our Cromwell—who now returns
Triumphant from the North.

SIXTH CITIZEN.

　　　　　　　　Let the poor king
Pass privately to Windsor—admiring crowds
Will yet attend his way.

SEVENTH CITIZEN.

　　　　　Ay, ay, his way to heaven or—

SEVERAL CITIZENS.

All hail to Cromwell !—Cromwell comes—Cromwell,
Our hope, our trust.

　　CROMWELL *enters, with Soldiers and great state.*]
　　　　　Thanks—thanks,
My friends and fellow-soldiers in the Lord ;
　3

The fight is fought, the victory is ours.
Praise and thanks to Him, the God of battles,
Who smiled upon our arms; not unto me—
His humble instrument.　Give thanks, give thanks!

TROOPS AND CITIZENS.

Amen!　Amen!　Amen!

IRETON.

Onward, brave troops.
　　　　　[*Soldiers and Citizens exeunt.*
To CROMWELL.]—General, the King has gone to Windsor.

CROMWELL.

Is sent, you mean—[*Aside.*]—and THENCE!!
To IRETON.]—Bid Whitelock, Widdington, Lenthal, and
　　Dean
Unto a private conference.

IRETON.

Where?

CROMWELL.

Where?　Where but here, at Whitehall?
　　　　　　　　　　[*Exit* IRETON.
Charles at Windsor!　Cromwell at Whitehall!
Charles king in title, but in power how fallen!
And I, Oliver Cromwell, master of this realm.
It is a vain and idle thing in me
To strive to keep my thoughts among the herd,
When all will have me great.　It has been whispered
That the King must die; some men of blood,
Warriors austere, who've ruled the nation
Now for many months, meditate a fearful vengeance
On the captive King.*　Where was engendered

* History of Independency　Part II.

This most horrid thought?　Where could it be
But in his most unrighteous acts, who, wrong
On wrong upon his people heaping, has reared
A power crushes beneath its might all reverence
And all love.　I will not harp on this,
Nor ever will consent to shed that royal blood—
A deed inexpiable, and which will move
The grief and horror of the world.　Some call
Me hypocrite; I am no fool.　Charles the First
Dead—vengeance all wreaked—his·faults all flown
With him, Charles the Second—next of the royal line—
Will rise in youth and innocence, and veiling
All his father's faults, that sainted blood will cry
Aloud to Heaven for vengeance on his judges.
I ne'er will sanction this, have I but power
To save him.*　　　　　　　　　　[*Exit* CROMWELL.

SCENE SECOND.

Scene changes to Room in Whitehall.—A Royal Bed.—WHITELOCK,
WIDDINGTON, LENTHAL, and DEAN, writing at a table.

CROMWELL *enters.*

ALL.

General, you are welcome once more to London.

CROMWELL.

Thanks, my friends, thanks.　Would that myself
Were the less kindly greeted, and my poor King
· Had but his measure of his people's love.

WHITELOCK.

General, that thought was idly born, though born
In reverence; nothing will now suffice
But—

* Heath.

CROMWELL, *throwing himself upon the royal bed.*

Nay, name it not; there ever are expedients left,
Asked in sincerity in a virtuous cause,
Heaven-sent.   I would devise some plan
For the return of the secluded members
To their duty in Parliament.   An answer
Of the Lower House to the messages of the army,
Counselling gentleness, and a Proclamation
Drawn, to be issued by the Lords and Commons
For the settlement of the nation.   I pray you
Have this speedily done.   [*Exeunt.*

CROMWELL, *alone.*

What am I now to do if this should fail?
I would not that his royal head should fall;
And yet it may not reign.   The people all are mine;
The soldiers too; but only mine while I am
Charles's foe.   Thus far has Heaven smiled
Upon the Independents' cause—a cause
By their forbearance sacred made; but let
That royal blood be spilt, each drop that falls
Will cleanse out an offence.
My Ironsides name must e'er untarnished be;
In our rare camp, no drunkenness or gambling e'er is seen;
No rights of peaceful citizens disturbed,
And woman's honor is most sacred held.
Hampden and Pym are in their graves—
Alas for England, and for me!—Hampden fell   [genets,
On Chalgrave field, and Pym now sleeps with the Planta-
While Buckingham, Strafford, Laud, lie in their bloody
        graves.

IRETON *enters.*

General, a missive—   [*Handing a letter.*

CROMWELL.

Nay, a letter.

IRETON.

'Tis from the Queen.

CROMWELL.

The Queen! what Queen?. This curse of queens
Has brought his royal head unto the block!
Ireton, my son, I see it all.
It shows as black as yonder stormy cloud,
And laden with Heaven's wrathfulness.
They shall not kill my King.   He yet shall live.
What would this Queen?

IRETON.

A pass to return to England.

CROMWELL.

Nay, nay, that would be fatal.   Her Popish name
Would whet the axe.   Her presence give the blow.

IRETON.

The States of Holland, too, have interposed.

CROMWELL.

Unwisely done; they have interposed ere now
As England's foes—this is too fresh in memories
Of the people and the troops.

IRETON.

Colonel John Cromwell,
Commissioned by the Prince of Wales,
Would wait on you.

CROMWELL.

Go tell him I may not see him.
Tell him I know his errand.   He knows

I would have saved my King—would he have saved
Himself—will save him if I may.   [*Ireton exits.*
I see it all; there is but one man left in England,
The world asserts it; that man is—who?
One Oliver Cromwell, late a plain country gentleman.
What trick would Fortune play me?   Fortune,
.The heathen's boast.   In this enlightened age,
The Scriptures teach, man has no fortune
But a destiny; clothed with due powers,
Guided by an almighty hand, so long
As Virtue's plain ways and walks, by Conscience
Sentinelled, are trod, no foes can come,
And his great charge fulfilled; God's appointed end
Is reached.
            If in his trust he fails, he falls
Forever; if he is true, he lives till the doom
Of time.
            There is a leaden weight about my heart;
A pall enshrouds my thoughts.
May Heaven give me strength in this dread hour.

BRADSHAW enters.

General, there is no treating with this Charles.
He will be King, or nothing.

HARRISON AND GRIMSHAWE *enter.*]

HARRISON.
                        That shall he be
Before to-morrow's sun.

CROMWELL, rising and advancing.
                        Nay, nay, my masters!
Such unseemly haste betokens malice, not justice.
Since 'tis your will his royal head must bow
To dust, remember he has been our King.
Let this our deed, at which the world shall stand

Amazed, at least the semblance of justice wear.
Deposed, dethroned, tried in the face of all the world,
For wrongs against his people and his realm,
He as a KING should die,—a warning
For all after times.

      Remember, He whose servitors
We are, was by the accursed unbelievers
Dragged unto His ignominious and most bitter death;
Remember how Nature yawned; how the sun
Shrunk from earth, in horror at the sight;
And the whole world convulsed. Remember, too,
How, God Himself, He rose; how His blessed name
Drowns every sound where'er 'tis heard, when
Every head in reverence bows, and every knee is bent;
How they, in theirs, are wretched wanderers through the
   wide, wide world,—
No land, no home, not even one resting-place!
I counsel, that you ponder well on this,
Lest that, too late, you learn your fatal error.

HARRISON.

General, are you against us? The troops—

CROMWELL.

          Are MINE!

BRADSHAW.

General, sign here our sentence—

CROMWELL.

Our sentence!—nay, nay!—not mine, not mine!
Oh! I would stay your suicidal hands;
You know not what you do!   [*Exit* CROMWELL.

BRADSHAW.

Our General not with us? Have we raised
A power we may not curb?

HARRISON.

I'll hasten, and stir up
The troops; if they demand it, he will yield.
His heart is with us, 'tis his hand that fails.

GRIMSHAWE.

It never failed till now.   He would not have
Us act so unadvisedly.   'Tis for ourselves,
Not Charles, he counsels this.   Let but the people
And the troops require, and he will sign the sentence.

BRADSHAW.

Then each unto his several friends; insist
Upon our sentence being passed; and executed
Without delay.   [*Exeunt.*

SCENE THIRD.

Cromwell's Room.

CROMWELL, *alone.*

Is it come to this? that I, who ever sought
But paths of peace and righteous ways, must steep
My soul in blood, or lose my life?   There's nothing left
But this.   My life! and what is life, that I should weigh it
Against eternal death—deepest damnation—
For this murder foul—for murder sure it is!
Who comes?--[IRETON *enters.*]—Ireton, my son, what
    means this haste?

IRETON.

The troops are murmuring that you stay their will;
The populace cry out, that they will have his blood.

CROMWELL.

So have they cried before from the oldest time,

Yet rent the air (their act scarce o'er) with wailings.
Ireton, my son—Charles the First dead, Charles the
    Second
Lives, most potent of the twain.   Charles the First
Living (imprisoned, an' you will), there is no Charles the
    Second,
And the Commons are rulers of the realm!

IRETON.

The Commons now are rulers of this realm—
Cromwell their General—soon their KING.
                    [CROMWELL *starts at this.*
For we, your troops, are masters of the land.

CROMWELL, *looking earnestly, fixedly, and sternly at* *IRE-
    TON, *goes up to him.*

There have been spectres, witches, weird women,
In the olden times, so teach the nursery dames;
Which of all these art thou?—wouldst drag my soul
To ruin, offering thus the diadem
For a blood-stained hand?   Canst thou be Ireton?—
My son?   Father to those darling babes
Caressing, fondling, call me grandsire?
My daughter's husband?—art a man?   Put out
Thine hand,—'tis flesh and blood!   Let me but gaze
Upon that face,—those locks;—they live, as I have seen
Them in the battle fierce, bristling with fury.
Those eyes,—so cold, so china-like,—are thine.
There are no smiles.
    [*Half aside.*]   I never saw a smile upon his face.
This hand—this cold and clammy hand—   *   *   *
How didst thou win my daughter's love?   Nay, nay,
Hast thou not entwined thyself about my heart?
Thy serpent beauties sure are basalisks!   *   *   *

        * Ireton, "the man of blood"—*Clarendon.*
    3*

*The vision, Ireton, said not I should be King,
But "*greatest* man of England."

IRETON.

                              How such, but King?—
See, here is Grimshawe.

GRIMSHAWE, *entering.*

                              General, the people
All, with one accord, demand his death.

CROMWELL.

Grimshawe, the troops are there to preserve
The law, which knows no populace
And no partisans.

HARRISON, *entering.*

General, the troops are with the tradesmen siding,
And all demand his death.
Here is the warrant, wanting but your signature.

CROMWELL.

Is it come to this?—leave it, pray leave it!
Leave me all, awhile.
        [*Exeunt all, save* IRETON, *who goes to one side.*
    RICHARD CROMWELL; *enters.*]
Ha! what wouldst thou, son? Com'st *thou* to urge
This bloody act? Why am I thus encircled by fierce
        hearts?

RICHARD CROMWELL.

Father, you are o'erwrought—you mistake my purpose.

CROMWELL.

Nay, nay! you, like the rest, would rather be great
Than good. I tell you, Virtue's is the only crown
That's worth the wearing.

* Clarendon.

RICHARD.

So have I learned,
From the first lesson that I conned with you
Till this dark hour of melancholy tasks.
Father, upon my knee I do beseech you, sign not that!
I'd rather toil from sun to sun in the far
Western wilds,—the turf my couch, the sky my canopy,—
Than have this dear hand stained by an unworthy act,
Much less give warrant for our monarch's death.

CROMWELL, *embracing him.*

Richard, my son—thou art my son—indeed
Thou art; I never prized you at one-half
Your worth. [*Seeing* IRETON.] Ireton, he reads a lesson
Unto you, and them—those bloody men.

IRETON.

He knows not the world.   He is too young—
The age of lovers, when, with mincing steps,
They track fair maids, with silvery tongues;
This their high ambition.

Here comes your fairest daughter.

CROMWELL.

Go ye, and learn the people's and the soldiers' wills;
I would be alone with her.

[IRETON *and* RICHARD *exeunt.*
It may be she would unfold the delicate leaves
Of her young heart unto her father's love,
As doth the tender flower to the ever-cheering sun.
ELIZABETH *enters.*]   My dearest child!

LADY ELIZABETH.

Father, your looks are sad, your eye is heavy,

And on your brow the clouds of care, not anger!
Half aside.]   I augur well from this.

CROMWELL.

Why so! what wouldst thou ask?

LADY ELIZABETH.

A life!

CROMWELL.

A life!   Whose is it that I hold the tenure of?
Sure I am grown great, when life is in my gift—
But I ne'er sought this power.

LADY ELIZABETH.

My King's.

CROMWELL.

Alas! it is not mine to give or keep.
All that I may do I have done; I am no longer
Master of myself, but slave to thousands.
Hark to the rabble's cry!—a cry for blood;
Hark to the murmurs of my troops!
Most melancholy sounds that ever fall
Upon a leader's ear.

LADY ELIZABETH.

Better hear this
Than Conscience's upbraiding voice should break
The silence of the midnight air, bearing
The shrieks of mothers, daughters, children grown,
Ay, infants, too, ever to your restless couch.

CROMWELL.

Stay! stay!   No more—no more!

LADY ELIZABETH.

One thing, and I have done:
You ever said, you loved me best of all.

I have loved you as never other loved;
And I would make you partner in my young heart's hopes,
Which you may turn to joy or bitterness
Which shall it be?   It is your daughter,
Father, asks you this.   One word, and life and love,
Or misery till death!

CROMWELL.

Nay, nay! how so?   Speak, speak!

LADY ELIZABETH.

I love our Liege's son, and he loves me;
His father saved—and thou canst do it—
Your daughter his son's bride—my father lives
In honor and in glory; the glory
Of a great, a virtuous deed!

Spurn this base rule;
'Tis but a mob's, who'll turn against you,
Gratified or no.

CROMWELL.

But Charles has sought my life—would seek it again—
And with my life my country's liberties.
Great Brutus slew his best friend for Rome;
Should Cromwell do less for England, thou noble girl?

LADY ELIZABETH.

Ay, father, this is true; but, Cæsar slain,
Was not the curse of blood upon their heads,
And early, ignominious deaths their lot?
'Twere best to ponder on it.   Oh, now I see
You're moved!   Give me that hideous paper,
Whose words gleam out like peace-pursuing fiends.

CROMWELL.

Nay, touch it not!   If Charles and England

Both can live, he shall; if one must die,
His was the smallest evil of the two.
The times, my child, are changed—

                              England is new-born.
The spirit of the far Western clime new nature
Has infused into us all.   We must move on,
Untrammelled by old customs, which do bind
The hands, as Popery binds the soul.
The Priest has fallen! The Spirit of the Lord
Is in the land; and where He is, there is Liberty.
Daughter, I would that I might grant thy prayer;
This Charles is e'en a noble boy; if I may save
His father, child, I will.   First England—then ourselves.
But hark! what notes are these?—a funeral dirge—
What other of the heroes of the age has fallen?
    IRETON *enters.*]
To ELIZABETH]—Daughter, pray retire.

                              [ELIZABETH *exits.*
Speak, Ireton, speak! what means your grief?

IRETON.

Cromwell, my father! you are a soldier,
And a Christian, too.   Rally around you
All your strength, for you have need of it.
The bolt has fallen on your house.

CROMWELL.

My house? my house?   My son! my son!
Where is my Oliver?

HARRISON, GRIMSHAWE, *and others enter, escorting a bier.*
What noble form is this?   My child's!   [*Falls on it.*
Almighty God, have mercy on me now.
My boy! my boy! speak, speak!—no voice to answer
Mine, that ne'er was heard in vain.

Hushed is the sweetest music I e'er heard ;
Fallen the noblest form I e'er beheld.

HARRISON.

General—

CROMWELL.

Can ye not spare me but a little while,
My masters?   Surely, the State's service
Gives me time to weep my first-born,
And most fondly loved.   How happened this,
And where?

HARRISON.

    Hastening to London with a small force,
Sir John Elliott, with a troop of the late King's Horse,
Assailed him.   A Cromwell living, he a Cromwell
Died—most bravely fighting to the last.
Upon the news being brought, I hastened
With full force, and found my boy—
For he was mine, as yours—all England's—
For all loved him—honored him.

        His murderer
Is ours—is to die ere set of sun.   His purpose
Was to hold your Oliver a hostage for the King.
The King suggested this ; so say these lines.

    [*Showing* CROMWELL *the papers.*

CROMWELL.

In Charles's hand !   Give me the warrant;
Blood will have blood.   He who slew the son
Can have no mercy at the father's hand.

    [*Signs the Warrant; then kneels by the bier.*
My son ! my son !

TABLEAU.

Curtain Falls.

END OF ACT III.

ACT IV.

SCENE FIRST.

The House of Commons.—The Statue of CHARLES thrown down, and on
its pedestal written, " The Tyrant, the last of the Kings, is gone."—In
session.

BRADSHAW AND GRIMSHAWE *advance.*

BRADSHAW.

So amazement sits upon the land, and discontent
Broods everywhere.

GRIMSHAWE.

   'Twas thus that Cromwell,
Who now is away in Ireland in our service,
Told us it would be, and charged upon us
Moderation.

BRADSHAW.

  He signed the warrant for King Charles's death.

GRIMSHAWE.

Who had not done the same, like circumstanced?
Open and secret threats—letters anonymous—his son
  thus sacrificed.

BRADSHAW.

He who foresaw the storm, should best know
How to still it.
   A resolution has passed the Commons,
That as the Lords seceded during the trial
Of their King, so henceforth we shall make
No more addresses to them, nor receive
Aught from them; that, as the existence
Of the Upper House is not only useless,

But dangerous, it ought forthwith to be abolished.
I also move the extinction of monarchical
Government in England, and declare it
High treason to proclaim, or any otherwise
Acknowledge Charles Stuart, commonly called
Prince of Wales.
　　　　　Let all in favor now in silence rise.
　They all rise, uncovered.]

BRADSHAW.

The Lord doth smile upon our acts.
Amen.

ALL.

　Amen.

BRADSHAW.

Hereto, then, I affix our great seal, whereon
Is inscribed—" On the first year of freedom,
By God's blessing restored, 1648."
Let now a Council of State be formed,
To consist of forty-one members, of whom
I do propose that Cromwell, Fairfax, St. John,
And the younger Vane shall be; upon them
Shall devolve all the duties which formerly
Attached to the Crown and its ministers
In the two Houses.

GRIMSHAWE.

　　　I would add you, friend Bradshaw,
To the same, and now do put it to the vote.

SPEAKER.

All in its favor rise.　　　　　　[*They rise.*
Our Government is formed, and we adjourn.　[*Exeunt.*

SCENE SECOND.

Whitehall.

LADY CROMWELL, LADY ALICE LAMBERT, LADY
ELIZABETH CROMWELL.

LADY ALICE.

Dear Lady Cromwell, hast thou no news from Ireland?
Some three months have already passed;
No tidings could be trusted from your Lord
And mine.

LADY CROMWELL.

      No news direct, but rumors of success;
Success such as has ever crowned
Our Cromwell's arms. Come, my fair Elizabeth,
Thy song, thy voice, should be attuned to joyful measures,
Thou peerless child of greatness.

LADY ELIZABETH.

             Nay, of griefs!
There is no balm in gold or grandeur
To the wounded heart; mother, I have not sung
For months, except his dirge.

LADY CROMWELL.

      Fie, fie! why must thou be
A puling girl, and weep for thy boy lover,
Forgetful of the greatness that surrounds thee?

LADY ELIZABETH.

Mother, thou hast crossed o'er the stream
Upon whose bosom Love's bark floats, and left
Its flowery banks for the thick chaparral,
Where the acactus, with its gorgeous hues,
Hides the sharp stings await the venturous foot.

This gorgeous grandeur blinds your eye sedate;
Fear lest its dazzling glories lead to ruin.

LADY CROMWELL.

Thou bird of evil omen! yet most fair
Of my fair brood, why flew the barb from the sole quiver
Could most deeply wound, that pierced thy bosom—
A wound must rankle, never to be healed by him?
Nay! cheer thee, child; there are a hundred heroes
Woo thy hand; ay, titled, and with wide domain,
Thou shouldst be mother to a race of men;
I would be grandam to the sweetest crew
That ever revelled o'er a gay parterre.

LADY ELIZABETH.

You might have been grandam to a long line
Of kings!

LADY CROMWELL.

　　And will be yet.

LADY ELIZABETH.

The dream was to my father, and no more.
Attendant enters.]

PATIENCE.

Madam, some gentlemen await on you.

LADY CROMWELL.

My Lady! Girl—will you never learn? admit them;
Daughter, receive them graciously.
　　BRADSHAW, GRIMSHAWE, *and* MARTIN *enter.*]
Ah, worthy Master Bradshaw, and my friends,
Grimshawe and Martin; your smiles betoken news—
Good news; haste give it me!

LADY ALICE.

And me; for I am trembling with loving eagerness.

BRADSHAW.

Temperance, fair dame, is next to chastity
In maiden hearts.

LADY CROMWELL.

Pray ye, what says my Lord?

BRADSHAW.

That Ireland is ours—Drogheda, Wexford,
Duncannon, Waterford, Estionage, Carrick,
And Passage Fort are won. The first-mentioned
Four, with loss of life; the last, surrendered.
All of your friends are well; Lord Broghill
Did good service to our cause, and the wild Irish
Fell.

LADY ALICE.

It was Lord Cromwell's voice that won him over.

LADY ELIZABETH.

My father's voice was ever wisest.

BRADSHAW.

Sweet child
Thou sayest well, and soon may thank him for us all;
I'd have no sweeter spokesman than yourself,
To render him the homage of our hearts.

LADY CROMWELL.

Why soon?   Surely the war is not yet over.

BRADSHAW.

His services are needed nearer home;
The Parliament have summoned him;
Our General Ireton is with him now,
And well may take command, though Cromwell has
Full liberty to appoint whom best it pleases him.
The Council waits, and we must take our leave.

LADY CROMWELL.

Farewell, gentlemen. My thanks to you.
                         [*Exeunt Gentlemen.*
Sweet Lizzy, see—I am mother of great men,
If not of kings: " Our General Ireton !"
I would that Richard loved an active life,
Not pondering o'er dull tomes—a carpet knight.
Alas! my Oliver! He was a hero from his birth.

A trumpet and people's cheers.

LADY ALICE.

Hark ye, the shouts! It is our General comes.

CROMWELL *enters, saluting each.*

My honored wife, my Lady, and my love—
How glorious shine your beauties at this hour;
A joyous greeting for your truant Lord.

LADY CROMWELL.

Who should have come with lute upon his arm.
Such sweet words on his lips. How fare you,
My dear Lord ?

CROMWELL.

             A little weary, though right well.
How does our honored Lambert's lovely wife ?
He bade me bear you this.   [*Kissing her.*
                   I need not ask ;
A garden of sweetest flowers by moonlight seen
Scarce rivals you.

LADY ·ALICE.

             Nay, pardon me, but rather
By the light of yon bright orb, just resting
Now upon the throne of day—a herald
Unto thee, our General and our Lord, it shows thy way.

CROMWELL.

Be but a harbinger of peace, and I shall thank
You, sweet one.
    Turning to Elizabeth.]—My fairest child,
Where is thy smile—thy kiss ?

LADY ELIZABETH, *kissing him.*

There, my *great* father—pardon me!

CROMWELL.

                            What means
This coldness in you, who ever rushed
Into my arms—or stood on tiptoe, eager
To embrace, when stayed in your approach ?
What! can it be that I am grown so proud
And great (if I am, I did not know it),
That even my best-loved daughter is awe-filled ?
If so—away with honors, glories, fame, and power—
I'd rather rule by love than majesty.   [*Turns away.*

LADY CROMWELL.

Nay, she has grown timid, Sir, of late ;
She sings no more—nor smiles.
Aside to ELIZABETH.]   Thou foolish girl!

CROMWELL.

                        I see it all.
Farewell, domestic joys—the innocent joys
Of home!
My generalship I purchased
With my dear son's blood ; my country's safety,
With my daughter's love!
Why, what a bawble is aggrandizement !
The serpent eye of Jealousy—the soft voice of Deceit—
The blandishments of men who favors seek—
Eye-service everywhere—but nothing from the heart !

I had it once—all that the heart could ask :
My son's, my daughter's. Charles stole his life ;
His son, her love—I know not which the weightiest loss :
Hers, 'tis a lighter grief to miss him here, a warrior
In heaven—than see her like a delicate flower
Lose her bloom, and perish leaf by leaf—
My girl ! My boy ! my brave, my noble boy,
My Oliver—why should I weep ?   He serves
In heaven now, while I am serving Heaven
Upon earth.
     I must attend upon the Council.

Exeunt Ladies the other.]   [*Exit one side.*

SCENE THIRD.

Grand Council-Chamber, Westminster—Counsellors seated—A Trumpet.

BRADSHAW.

Hark to the trump !   Our General comes ;
He has proved himself a gallant officer—
The General of the age.

GRIMSHAWE.

     As he has proved
Best Counsellor in our cause—
     Welcome unto our General !

As CROMWELL *enters, with Officers and armed Attendants,
the Counsellors rise.*

CROMWELL.

Thanks, my good masters—fellow-Counsellors !
Thanks for this welcome of my humble self,—
The honored instrument of Heaven's will,
To whom all honor, power, glory, is given.

They all uncover their heads.]

BRADSHAW.

On earth as heaven.   Amen.

CROMWELL.

Our arms victorious—Ireton, my son,
I have left in Ireland, supreme.
In all my sieges, battles, storms, assaults,
I deemed that mercy best would. be consulted
By speediest termination to our war,
And therefore pray ye think, if you would harshly judge
My course,
" How much the evils attend
Upon a few instances of severity
In the outset, are compensated
By the cutting off long years of obstinate resistance."
Finding the Irish such a wild and savage race,
I felt that I was forced to string myself
Even to acts of seeming cruelty and horror;
Their arms not turned upon their foes,
They turn upon each other—with scarce a cause of wrong.

GRIMSHAWE.

In Henry the Second's reign, Cambrenses
Wrote—"that the only way to civilize
The Irish was to exterminate them
And seize their estates."

CROMWELL.

                    Nay, my good masters!
I would not have that Emerald Isle,
The great capital out of which our debts
Are paid, our services rewarded, our acts
Of bounty performed.   Win them to peace
And love, by gentlest arts; now that they, knowing,
Fear your power, teach them that 'tis not your intention

To extirpate the nation—for now in flight
They seek a refuge from their wrongs ; at least
Some fifty thousand have already left the land.
I would that they were taught the peaceful arts,
Then plenty soon would follow in their train,
Poverty be a stranger to that land, most blessed
On earth, and virtue reign lord paramount.

BRADSHAW.

We will debate on this, and act as you may counsel.
But now we have received news from Scotland :
They have proclaimed young Charles their King,
And King of England, Ireland, and France.

CROMWELL.

But have they made him such ?   Best as it is—
Better that now while our troops are flushed
With victory.   Trouble not, my masters ;
We will dispel their force as sun the mist.

BRADSHAW.

Thou dauntless man—now learn what for thy services
The House appoints.   [CROMWELL *bows*.
The Palace of St. James thy residence,
With such attendants as beseemeth thee
And them; large grants of land
                                        To their victorious General,
Most full approval of your every step,
And, with entire confidence in your ability
And faithfulness, they, on behalf of all England,
Give their thanks.

CROMWELL.

    Nay, my good friends, Whitehall is well enough.

BRADSHAW.

For you, 'tis true, who love the tented field.

CROMWELL.

Nay, would I were out of the trade of war,
And here in council with you at Westminster.

BRADSHAW.

Till then thy wife and children are our most valued
　　　guests;
While you are caring for the State away,
Here must we guard thèm cheerily.
　　　　　　　　　　　　We have sent
To learn Lord Fairfax's will as to the conduct
Of the war in Scotland, and he declines
Assuming the command—'tis thought, at instance
Chiefly of his Presbyterian wife; but says
That should the Scots England invade, he would be ready
To lay down his life.

CROMWELL, *aside.*

　　　　　　　How all things tend to my advancement;
I could devise naught better.
Aloud.]　"Notwithstanding his unwillingness, I pray
Ye may continue him General of your army,
For I would rather serve under him, than command
The greatest army in all England."

LUDLOW.

　　　　　　　　　　　Fearing your views
Were such, we've sent a committee to advise
With him.　　　　　　　　　[CROMWELL *going.*
　　　　　I pray you do not withdraw yourself,
Nor yet, in compliment and humility,
Obstruct the public service by your refusal.
Stay yet awhile, and learn what Lord Fairfax
Further says; our committee come.

COMMITTEE *enter.*

　　　　　　　Still on his purpose bent,

Lord Fairfax's Secretary at the door awaits
To surrender his commission, if we
Think fit to receive it.

CROMWELL.

                    Did ye remind
Him that the Scots had invaded England
Since the recognition of the solemn League
And Covenant, and in direct contravention
Of its letter as well as spirit; that now
They meditate another inroad, under the banners
Of Charles Stuart, whom, without the Commonwealth's
          consent,
They have proclaimed Sovereign of the three kingdoms;
And therefore if there must be war, 'twere best
To choose the enemy's country for the scene,
Than permit a hostile army to penetrate
Into the heart of this nation, already wasted
By the ravages of our own civil dissensions?

COMMITTEE.

We did, my Lord.   He still refused.

CROMWELL.

Then, my masters, if ye do receive surrender
Of his commission, which I would counsel
Ye temperately to consider, though *I* know not
What else to do, since he will die to all his former glory,
"And become the monument of his own name,"*
Which every day'll wear out, there should
For his past services recompense be made
     Aside.]   (Their future General may require the like),
A liberal recompense.

BRADSHAW.

So let it be; receive we the commission,

          * Cromwell's words.

And grant to him two thousand pounds a year.

LUDLOW.

Two thousand pounds!—scarce enough, my friend; for
    you or us
It would suffice.

CROMWELL.

       Greatness, my masters, brings
Great charges in its train; make it five thousand pounds
    a year;
Now, I pray ye, excuse me.   [*Retires one side.*

BRADSHAW.

Our General counsels well; so let it be.
Admit his Secretary.
   Secretary enters.]   Young Sir, we do accept
Surrender of your Lord's commission;
Bear this to him, with our best thanks—
A settlement upon him for his past services
Of five thousand pounds a year: so would our General
    Cromwell.
This being disposed of, now I would propose
That our Lieutenant-General be Captain-General
Of all the land forces; that his commission
Be instantly drawn up; and that the Council of State
Hasten the preparations for the Northern expedition.

ALL.

Let it be so.

BRADSHAW.

      The commission is prepared; I will affix
The seal. Captain-General, I salute you—now—my friend!
CROMWELL *bows to them, when they retire, and then ad-
    vances with commission in his hand.*

CROMWELL.

Captain-General of all the land forces of England,

Then supreme ruler, under Heaven, of the realm!
Why am I raised to all this honor?   I sought it not.
It must be that I am by high Providence
Selected for the accomplishment of great purposes;
" May it not be as instrument of the will divine,
As writ in Holy Scripture, which shadows forth
The triumphs and felicities of the Messiah's kingdom?"
    LUDLOW *enters.*]   Ha! Ludlow, my friend!
    Aside.]   I do not understand this man.

LUDLOW.

                                        General.

CROMWELL.

Thou art cold—why so?   Hast thou suspicion
Of my integrity, as servant of the public?
Dost thou suppose that I would be their master,
Seeing I am grown so great in power?
Believe me, I am but Heaven's instrument.

LUDLOW.

Enough, enough! I should not doubt you.

CROMWELL.

No, you should be the very last to do so.
Incumbent it may be on me many things to do,
Even extraordinary in the judgment of some men,
Who, now opposing, would bring ruin on themselves,
On me, as well as on the public cause.
But here I do declare that all I do
Shall be but for the people's good, for whose welfare
I am prepared to sacrifice my life.

LUDLOW.

We may not doubt you, General, in this.

CROMWELL.

You should not, with the past proofs you have;
All my desires are to settle the nation
In a free and equal commonwealth.
There are no other means to keep the old rulers out;
And, in all reverence and humility, I must say
I feel it is the Lord's design His people
To deliver from every burden.
His will and wise decrees to me I read
In " that the Lord at thy right hand shall strike
Through kings in the day of His wrath;
He shall fill the places with the dead bodies;
He shall wound the heads over many countries;
The people shall be willing in the day
Of *thy power*—thou art a priest forever."
There have I my commission. I will reform
The clergy and the law; the sons of Zeruiah
Are still too strong for us.
                            Wilt thou not aid me
To fulfil God's will?   I need the services
Of such as thou, godly and gallant gentlemen.

LUDLOW.

Most gladly, General, if in God's service.

CROMWELL.

It is; wilt thou accept the Lieutenant-Generalship
Of Ireland?

LUDLOW.

        I will—most sensible of the honor
You now do me.

CROMWELL.

        Then hasten preparation.

Ireton has returned, and I would you were there.
Farewell.   [*Exit* LUDLOW.
          He may be troublesome.   I would remove—
During my absence in the North, where, should reverse
Befall me—the more violent republicans,
Of whom he is one; they might take advantage,
And place the power of the State in other hands.
Oh, curse of greatness!—I do already feel
That I have more to dread from former friends
Than enemies avowed.
                    The army I will make
Subservient to my ulterior plans;
I'll separate the interests of the soldiers
From those of their old commanders;
I will dismiss many of the " godly party,"
And give their places to men who make
Arms their trade.
While Fairfax stands an empty name, I'll mould the army
To my mind—" weed out the godly," they are
Bad fighting men, and fill their rooms with such
As make no question for conscience' sake ;*
But I must do it gently, and unperceived
By the eyes of men.   I need no " agitators;"
They are as two-edged swords—I must not cast
Them only to one side, but have them under foot,
And, if needs be, grind them into powder;
So shall I distribute all my fanatics far apart
In different regiments.
                    We will have
No convocations now of saints.
      IRETON *enters.*]   Ha, Ireton, what news?

                         IRETON.

Bad—as ever.
                  * Cromwell's words.

CROMWELL.

Give it me.

IRETON.

Three of our bravest captains are arraigned
For a conspiracy against your life,
And now are before the Council of State, in the
Adjoining chamber.

CROMWELL.

My life! what would they with my life?
They value it at more than I do, if they'd steep
Their souls in perdition—their good names
In infamy.
        Who are they, and their cause for it?

IRETON.

Rich, Staines, and Watson—they have confessed
That in a dream they were advised to it,
In words of Scriptural cant.

CROMWELL.

                In the adjoining chamber,
Do you say? Not yet condemned? I'll make
An example of them for all time. Come with me.
                                    [*Exeunt.*

SCENE FOURTH.

Room adjoining Council-Chamber.

RICH, STAINES, *and* WATSON, *before the Council.*

CROMWELL *enters with* IRETON.

What meaneth this, my good masters—and ye,
My well-tried captains, conspiracy against my life!
Why would ye take it before the eyes of men?

Ye who might have had it tens of thousand times,
Unseen by all save the unseen eye of God?
My body-guard, ever in the closest fight;
. Ye easily had mistook me for a foe;
My sentinels, at silent hour of night,
When all about me slept save ye yourselves—
Ay, and my very cup-bearer wert thou, my Rich,
When I was faint at Naseby—fie, fie, Sirs!
Shame on ye, pitiful, sneaking, and poor knaves
That ye are! see how ungrately ye had been to me—
How treacherous, cowardly to yourselves!
What would ye further with them, Sirs?

BRADSHAW.

A hempen cord!

CROMWELL.

   Your pardon, my good Bradshaw,
And my thanks, my friends, in that you deem
My life worth three—with your good leave, I have
A condign punishment for them.

BRADSHAW.

Pronounce it thou—against you their offence.

CROMWELL.

'Tis this: that ye be taken hence—what! do ye start
And tremble? ye poor weak fools! do ye fear
Death now? ye who ne'er knew fear before?
I have oft marked ye well, Sirs—I say, shall be taken
Hence—taken to my troops—all your bonds loosed—
Conscience awakened from this dreadful lethargy,
Ye shall your deed anticipated see
In all its naked horror—*upon the rack*—
Ye tremble—see what mean things a guilty conscience
Makes, e'en of the stoutest and the bravest hearts;—

4*

Upon the *rack*, I say—ay, upon the *rack*
Of *conscience* ye shall lie—a living testimony
Of my judgment, and show unto the world
The vengeance Cromwell takes upon his private foes.
But woe to those whom he shall find the State's.
Go hence, and let me hear no more of this.
When that ye deem my country needs my life,
Come then and take it—'tis freely hers.
Release their bonds.

BRADSHAW.

Thou great and glorious soul,
The State would thou shouldst have a private guard.

CROMWELL.

I have it, friends ; but in the private thoughts,
The secret heart of every Englishman.
With God upon my side, these canting fools
Will prove a better bulwark than ten thousand guards.
Now join in prayer and thanks to Heaven, my friends,
Then will I unto Scotland.

[*They kneel, and curtain falls.*

END OF ACT IV.

ACT V.

SCENE FIRST.

Council-Chamber.

BRADSHAW, GRIMSHAW, *and* MARTIN.

MARTIN.

What news to-day from Cromwell?

BRADSHAW.

Our foes dispersed at Derwent, Dunbar,
Indeed, where'er he met them; at Edinburgh,
He lies sick with a grievous fever;
Two skilful doctors to his aid I've sent,
And, by God's providence, I trust he may be saved.
The State can spare him not; though here he writes,
" Indeed, my Lord, your service needs not me—
I'm a poor creature, have been but a dry bone,
And am still an upnrofitable servant
To my Master and to you."   But, Heaven
Be praised! our Goddard writes, he mends;
And the same hour brings advice that the young Charles
In arms towards England comes.

GRIMSHAW.

                And this from Cromwell;
Which doth intimate that all his forces
Withdrawn beyond the Forth, temptation thus
Is thrown in Charles's way, to confide himself
And cause to the English nation, whose loyalty
He would test.
      He our General further entreats that we,

The Council of State, collect what force
We can without loss of time, and give Charles check
Until he shall o'ertake him.   Lambert, with the cavalry,
Is sent to join brave Harrison at Newcastle,
To watch their motions, and straiten them on their way,
Though not to risk a battle.
　　　Enter an officer.]　　　　　Ha! what news?

OFFICER.

Major-General Massy and the Earl of Derby
Have been repulsed by Lilburn at Wigan,
And Charles has entered Worcester, where
He has solemnly been proclaimed by the Mayor,
Amid the loud acclamations of the gentlemen
Of the county.

BRADSHAW.

Charles at Worcester!—haste ye and rouse our friends;
Bid them use all speed to meet our Cromwell,
And aid him in his " crowning victory;"
For such shall this fight be.   Haste ye, and urge on
Our supplies and men.   Haste all!　　　　[*Exeunt.*

SCENE SECOND.

Troop before Worcester.—Hour, Daybreak.

Troops enter and form in line of battle, crying, "Long live
the Commonwealth of England!" "Long live CROM-
WELL!" *who enters with* IRETON *and* OFFICERS.

CROMWELL.

Thanks, thanks, my brave friends and fellow-soldiers.
What news, my Ireton?

IRETON.

The Bridge of Upton, held by General Massy,
Lambert has carried against fearful odds,
Leaving their General wounded on the field.

TROOPS.

Praise be to God!—long live our gallant Lambert!

IRETON.

Fleetwood has forced the passage of the Team.
A bridge of boats over the Severn at Bernhill
Thrown; at Powick, too, a fierce attack was begun,
And pike to pike they fought at set of sun.

CROMWELL.

Day dawns, my troops—nay, 'tis the sun himself;
                    [*Sun breaks through clouds.*
Nature has veiled our brave intents;
So "let the Lord arise, and let His enemies
Be scattered."*

*Martial Music; cannon at first near, then more distant.
They charge upon the enemy ; fresh troops come on the
stage, and charge after charge.*

On, my brave troops! on! on!
They break—their King doth turn—Ha! ha! brave boys!
I profess they run.   The victory is ours;
The Commonwealth is safe.   Let all our thoughts
Tend to His honor, who hath wrought
So great salvation, and let not wantonness
And pride follow this crowning mercy.

OFFICER *enters and presents papers.*

OFFICER.

From the Council of State to their General Cromwell.
                            [*Retires.*

* Psalm lxviii

CROMWELL.

The fight is fought; the victory is gained;
The Scots subdued; *their* Charles the Second fled;
What now remains to do?—Much, much—there is
A war within this *heart*, far fiercer raging
Than all outward foes.   Down, fell ambition,
With your fiend-born crew, which feast upon its members
Ere 'twill die!
                    Now, as I have in arms,
So must I seek in peaceful arts to raise
The power of England.   ‘
    Looking at the papers.]   They do salute me here
As though I were their King, and would escort
Me in great state to London.   My home, a palace—
And in each address greet my ears with loftier adulation
Than e'er was lavished on the scion
Of an hundred kings!
    IRETON *enters.*]   Ha! Ireton—'twas bravely fought—
A word with you.
                    The power of Parliament
Must be lowered!—its duration limited—
All political offences committed
Before Worcester's fight must be forgiven,
Except some certain cases.

. IRETON.

This is well thought; 'twill make you friends.
It is decided Parliament be dissolved
Three years from this.   [*Exit.* .

CROMWELL.

                    Three years!—but see, here are

Enter WHITLOCK, WHALLY, DESBOROUGH.]

Our friends.   Ha! Whitlock, Whally, Desborough—

What think ye, Gentlemen—
Were it best to perpetuate the Commonwealth
On fixed principles, or re-establish a mixed form
Of monarchical government?

WHALLY.

General, our friends,
The army, will not have a Monarchy.

WHITLOCK.

I would advise revival of the ancient Constitution—
King, Lords, and Commons—'tis better adapted
Than a Republic to the laws, the habits,
The feelings of Englishmen.

CROMWELL.

Well spoken, learned friend,
But pray, whom would you recommend unto the throne?

WHITLOCK.

Charles Stuart or the Duke of York, provided
They submit to our conditions.

CROMWELL.

Aside.]   Humph! [*Aloud.*] Methinks
They never will. 'Tis true, somewhat
Of a monarchical government would be most effectual,
If it could be established with safety
To the liberties of the people as Englishmen
And Christians.
Methinks I have heard you do propose
Reduction of the army and of their pay.
By your leave, deem you this wise?—pray you,
Weigh it well, as also in all other retrenchments.
Rather let speedy and effectual means
Be taken for the propagation of the Gospel,

And all arrears due the army be paid forthwith.
Remember you their services and privations
In the course of a long war.

      See ye not, my friends,
That this paltry junto of statesmen who preside
At Westminster, the miserable remains
Of that illustrious body first met in 1640,
Actuated by no feelings but the love
Of power and emolument, intend
To keep the precious fruits of victory
To themselves, in their own hands, and condemn
The army to poverty and degrading insignificance?
'Twould be unjust, disgraceful, that men
Who never saw the tented field, nor suffered
In the long campaign, should enjoy
Those things for which the army have so often
Shed their blood.   Let them now be in possession,
They never will resign; but, in defiance
Of the people and our soldiery, exclude
From all share in the government every man
Of truly patriotic principles.

    Whally, pray you draw up a petition
To this effect, and vindicate your rights.

WHALLY.

We will.

DESBOROUGH.

 Ay, and hasten to present it.
   [*Exeunt* WHALLY *and* DESBOROUGH.

WHITLOCK.

General, may not this course be deemed,
To say the least, hasty and unconstitutional,
Thus to address the Parliament—in either hand
The sword or the Petition?

CROMWELL.

You, Whitlock, are a lawyer,
Who by your code must work; men of the world
And soldiers, let their natures teach.
You are a very faithful, most efficient Lord Commissioner,
But, I fear much, look not into the root of the times.
You have met our officers, learned their views—
" What think you, if a man should take upon himself
To be a king; would it not cure all ills ?"

WHITLOCK.

The remedy, I think, were worse than the disease.

CROMWELL.

Why think you so ?

WHITLOCK.

As to your own person,
The title of king would be of no advantage.
You have already the full kingly power.
It might awaken jealousies—besides,
The King of Scots yet lives ; the people look
Upon him as their natural King.

CROMWELL.

The King of Scots—[*Aside.*]—why died he not at Worcester ?

WHITLOCK.

I would propound your Excellency should send
To him, and have a private treaty with him;
Secure yourself and friends ; make you and your posterity
Forever great—the name of Cromwell an example
For all time.   He will accept any condition,—
Besides, there is a rumor in the land,
That there's a link binds Charles to Cromwell's House.
You have a daughter—pardon me—most fair ;

This Charles is young, and once did consort with her—

[CROMWELL starts.

Wherefore not wed them ?* Then your right to rule,
As his Prime Minister, no man could dispute.

CROMWELL.

He has already sought my daughter's hand ;†
But have I the right to jeopard my dear child's peace,
My country's honor and prosperity,
By trusting one so profligate, so prodigal,
So lost to all fair fame as he ?

I cannot think of it.

I have refused her hand.   Meantime, I would suggest
That the sovereign power be placed
In the hands of a Commission of forty persons,
Chosen from the Army, the Senate,
And the Council of State.   What think you of this ?
Some of our friends do counsel it.

WHITLOCK.

I fear

'Twere dangerous to dissolve the House; besides,
Your Excellency, the formation of the proposed Commis-
    sion
Is quite unconstitutional.

CROMWELL.

Ever the lawyer, Whitlock.

I thank you for your friendship, and when you have
Leisure from the cares of state, which I know
Weigh heavily on you, will further counsel take.
Good day, my friend—my honest friend.

[Exit WHITLOCK.

He wed my daughter !   That may not be.
'Twas by my act his father died.   This Whitlock

---

* Russell.   † Pictorial History of England.

Is very honest—the spokesman of the times.
None but a Stuart can, it seems, be king.
The vision said, I should be greatest man, but did not
    say *the King!*
We'll look to this.
    INGOLDSBY *enters.*]   Ha! Ingoldsby, my friend!

INGOLDSBY.

Advised of what your and the army's feelings
Are, the Commons now are urging through the Bill
For their own dissolution, encumbered
With all the provisions to which the military are opposed.

CROMWELL.

Did none object to this?   Had we no friends there?

INGOLDSBY.

Harrison most sweetly and most humbly
Conjured them to pause, while I came here
To counsel you to act.   Your presence is much
Needed there.

CROMWELL.

    Thou hast well done,—*now is the time*
To act. We'll hasten unto Westminster.
Call Colonel Worsley and my Guard.   [*Exeunt.*

SCENE THIRD.

House of Commons in session—Westminster.

CROMWELL *enters with* INGOLDSBY, *and takes his seat on*
one of the outer benches, and beckons to HARRISON.

CROMWELL.

Harrison, I judge the Parliament now ripe
For a dissolution.

To St. John.]   My friend, my friend, I have come
With a purpose of doing what grieves me
To my very soul, and what I have earnestly
With tears besought the Lord not to impose
On me; but there is a necessity, in order
To the glory of God and the good of the nation.

HARRISON.

Sir, the work is very great and dangerous.
I desire you seriously to consider before you
Engage in it.

CROMWELL.

You say well; we will consider on it.

SPEAKER.

The Bill for the dissolution of this House,
With due restrictions on the military power,
Having been well debated, I move the question
Now be taken.

CROMWELL (*to* HARRISON).

This is the time—now must I do it.
Addressing the House.] My friends, my friends, have we
        fought and bled for this?
Left we our homes, our wives, our babes, to make
The sward at best our beds, if not our graves,
While you, self-seekers and profane, denying justice,
And oppressors all, lapped in luxuries,
Found uneasy rest even upon your downy pillows—
We fasting when you feasted—the elements
Fiercest beating on our unprotected heads,
While you sat sheltered by your blazing hearths,
Idolizing the lawyers, constant advocates of tyranny?
And for what did we this?   Returning
Victorious over every foe, to find reward

In glory, honor, ease, and plenty?   Homes where
We might rest our wearied frames, and nurse
Our racked joints to health again?

                                       Was this our return?
No, no; not so; no comfort for your tools;
Months of our pay in arrears; our crying babes,
Crying but for the crumbs fall hourly from your tables;
Our weeping wives, heart-riven by their sufferings;
While we, disabled in your cause that ye might feast,
Have not wherewith to break our fast.   But, Sirs,
Your time has come.   The Lord has disowned you;
He has chosen more worthy instruments
To perform His work.

SIR HARRY VANE.

                   Sir, Sir, I never have heard
Words so unparliamentary and offensive,
And uttered, too, by our own servant,
Whom we have so fondly cherished; whom,
By unprecedented bounty, we have raised
To the elevation on which he now stands.

CROMWELL.

Come, come, Sir; I'll put an end to your prating.
This must not, shall not be.   Ye shall disgorge
A portion of those rights which ye so long
Have preyed on.   Ye would be masters; fit masters
Ye shall be, but of yourselves alone.
Here die your tyrannies, ambitions, robberies,
And oppressions of the public.

                Ho, there! without! [*Soldiers enter.*
BEHOLD YOUR MASTERS!   *I*, their and God's instrument,
For shame on you, vile leeches that ye are!
Go, get you gone; give place to honester men;
To those who will more faithfully discharge

Their trust.   You are no longer a Parliament!
I tell you, you are no longer a Parliament!
The Lord, the mighty Lord, has done with you;
He has chosen other instruments for His work.

SIR HARRY VANE.

I do protest against this proceeding.

CROMWELL, *laughing.*

Oh, Sir Harry Vane!   Sir Harry Vane!
A vain protest—most vain.   The Lord deliver me
From Sir Harry Vane—ha! ha! ha!
    Taking MARTIN *by the cloak.*]   Thou art a lecherous
      knave—retire;
We must have modest men here!
    To another.]   Thou art an adulterer—begone!
You taint the very air.
    To another.]   Thou art a drunkard and a glutton—
Away! a very beast!
    To another.]   And thou an extortioner–
The rack were thy just doom.   Millions hast thou
Kept on it.   God gave even you a conscience.
Go—for now you'll find it—go to your solitude.
I have your ill-gotten, heart-wrung gains.
Ye are dishonest and corrupt livers all,
A shame and scandal to the profession
Of the Gospel.

SPEAKER LENTHAL.

I do refuse to withdraw,
Unless I am compelled to leave this chair.

HARRISON *leads forth two of the military, at a sign from*
CROMWELL, *to make a show of force, and, laying his
hand on* LENTHAL, *assists him to descend.   About eighty,*

among whom is ALGERNON SIDNEY, *follow this example, and move towards the door.*

CROMWELL.

It is you who have forced me to do this.
I have sought the Lord night and day, that
He would rather slay me, than put me on
The doing of this work.

ALDERMAN ALLEN.

It is not yet too late
To undo what has just been done.

CROMWELL.

This from you, Sir?
You, who have defrauded the public to the amount
Of some hundred thousand pounds, as Treasurer
Of the army!   Take him into custody,
Until he answers for this peculation.
   Fixing his eyes on the mace.]
What shall we do with this fool's bawble?
Here—carry it away.
*He snatches the Act of Dissolution from the hands of
     the Clerk.*]
Lock fast the door, and bring the keys—
I will unto Whitehall.

[*He retires, and the door is locked.*

SCENE FOURTH.

Whitehall.—Council of State—Council of Officers waiting Cromwell's
return.

CROMWELL *enters.*

My friends, my fellow-soldiers, I have been sorely tried;
I did not think to have done what I did;

But, perceiving the Spirit of God
So strong upon me, I would no longer
Consult flesh and blood, but let the Spirit act.
Behold the spoil—the mace, the keys of the lower House,
The Act of Dissolution—the Parliament is no more.

OFFICER.

How mean you, General? The Parliament no more?
This course can only lead to ruin and confusion.

CROMWELL.

Leave that to me. Have I ever yet failed?
I will do much more good to the country
Than ever could be expected from Parliament.
Aside.] Ireton, a word with you. [*They retire one side.*

COLONEL OAKEY.

Means so hypocritical, the end will sure be bad.
What could be passing in the General's mind,
When he praised the Parliament so highly
To the Council of Officers, and yet proceeded
Immediately afterwards to eject them
With so much scorn and contempt?

DESBOROUGH.

True, true; if ever the General drolled in his life,
He has drolled now. We must look to this.

CROMWELL.

Gentlemen, if you are here met as private persons,
You shall not be disturbed; but if as a Council
Of State, this is no place for you; and since
You cannot but know all that was done at the House
But this morning, so take notice that the Parliament
Is dissolved.

BRADSHAW.

Sir, we have heard what you did
At the House in the morning, and before many hours
All England will hear it; but, Sir, you are mistaken
To think that the Parliament is dissolved;
For no power under heaven can dissolve them
But themselves.　Therefore take you notice
Of that.

SIR ARTHUR HAZELRIG.

Ay, indeed; this is true.

MR. LOVE AND MR. PEAT.

Ay, true; most true.

CROMWELL.

Ye too, Gentlemen!　I thank ye, Sirs.
All England soon will hear it; and, hearing, know
That the Parliament would have sent their officers
And soldiers into private life, upon diminished pay,
And stripped of all influence those who had made
Them great, and England to be feared.
The Army and the Navy both, in their addresses
Unto me, declare that they will stand or fall,
Live or die, in support of these my measures.
The populace throughout the land will thank me
For it; ay, and chant hymns of triumph
O'er your fall; magnify the name of the Lord,
Who has broken the mighty, and cast
The proud down to the ground.

Aside.]　　　　　　　　　　Ireton, 'tis well
We have done what we have; these statesmen
Are fast becoming adepts in our policy.
Had but the Bill for dissolution passed,
Those neuters—those, I mean, of the Presbyterian interest,
Who had not consented in our measures—

5

IRETON, *interrupting him.*

The King's death and the Army's measures.

CROMWELL.

Ireton, no more of that; name it not,
Name it not! When memory calls it up,
My heart is blanched, and what I have to do
I do by halves—those hated hours shadow
All my days.

IRETON.

The wisdom of your acts
Refutes all charges, and should dispel such thoughts.

CROMWELL.

It may be so; but enough of this.
By interposing my authority just when I did,
The dispute I limited to a body
Of men who, for reasons various, had ceased
To be longer popular—call it as you may,
My good fortune or my great political wisdom.
My friends, let now a Council of State
Be appointed, to watch over the peace and safety
Of the Commonwealth, and superintend
The present management of public affairs,
In number thirteen—nine military and four civilians;
A Scriptural number, and vouchsafed to us
By Him whom here we seek to serve. Sir Harry Vane,
Pray you be one of us.

SIR HARRY VANE.

· Thank you, General; though the reign
Of the saints is begun, I shall defer my share
Until I go to Heaven.

CROMWELL.

Or to —, as it best pleases you;

All have a right to choose their company.
   Beckoning them to one side.]
Good Major Salloway, and Carew, my friend,
Prithee, your care and counsel.   I know not how
I can sustain this weight now falls upon me.
Thoughts of the awful consequences make me tremble.
Free me, I prithee, from the great temptation
Laid before me.   Go ye, I pray, forthwith
Unto Chief-Justice St. John and Mr. Selden,
And together draw some instrument of government,
Which may take the power out of my hands.

SALLOWAY.

The way to free you from this temptation
Is for you not to look upon yourself
To be under it, but to rest persuaded
That the power of the nation is in the good people
Of England, as formerly it was.

CROMWELL.

                              Thou speakest well;
My many cares at times obscure my thoughts.
I pray you, then, summon our chief officers
To meet me at Whitehall forthwith, where they may
         consider
What 'twere best to do.

SALLOWAY.

         We will.

CROMWELL.

                              Do it forthwith.
'Tis well.   Some private business calls me now—
Prithee, attend to this. [*Exeunt* CAREW *and* SALLOWAY.
                   Ireton, read ye their thoughts?
We must be wary.

IRETON.

Ay, and bold; the power is yours.

CROMWELL.

And I will keep it. I will conclude the treaty
With the Portuguese Ambassador, suspend
The four Judges do offend, and make
Two new appointments; nominate new Commissioners
Of the Treasury and Admiralty; continue
The monthly assessments of one hundred and twenty
　　　thousand pounds
For an additional half year. For form's sake,
I will submit it to my Council of State;
It will sanction it in the eyes of England.
'Twere well, I think, too, for form's sake,
That we and our Council of State
Should nominate a Parliament
Of holy, pious men. Did our ministers
In the several counties send returns
Of persons faithful, fearing God,
And hating covetousness, who may be deemed
Qualified for this high and important trust?
I'll choose, say, an hundred and fifty to serve for certain
　　　places
In the three kingdoms.

IRETON, *showing a list.*

They did—are here—and I have chosen them.

CROMWELL, *laughing.*

'Tis well—a goodlie
If not Godlie company. There are an hundred and fifty,
　　　we,
That is, you, my Ireton, and I, know to be true
And faithful. You will observe

They did appear personally at Whitehall
On the *Fourth Day of July*, 1653—
This shall be hailed throughout the world
As Freedom's Birthday.   Attend on them;
Go you, and send me instant word how they conduct.
                                        [*Exit* IRETON.
   Enter the Quaker Merchant Fox.]
                              Most worthy friend,
What wouldst thou have?   A merchant prince,
Most honored of God's instruments—link
In the priceless chain of peaceful arts
That bind all climes together—source
Of England's glory—God's treasurer on earth—
Trustee immaculate of the wealth He gives,
In charity's sweet offices to dispense—
Mid heaviest charges e'er has Cromwell's ear.

                    FOX.

My ship from India—her cargo priceless—
Is by the Spaniards, in the Channel, taken.

                  CROMWELL.

Your ship!   Truly thou say'st her cargo's priceless—
'Twas England's honor that she convoyed hither.
And in the Channel too!—at our very doors!
But what matters that?   Were it in farthest seas,
Our flag should be immaculate.   Their wealth
Has made these Spaniards arrogant.
'Twill prove the curse and ruin of their land—
Misused, abused, the trust forgotten.
Thou shalt be recompensed ten days from this;
Make out your charges; 'tis England's cause;
Our Blake shall straightway seek their argosies.
Monuments of your goodness fill the land,
Which the most loses in your loss.

FOX.

My duty—nothing more—no praise in that—
My habit and my home I have—'tis all I need-
The rest is for the State.

            So do I humbly take my leave.

CROMWELL.

God's peace be with thee.   [*Exit Quaker* Fox.

An Officer enters and hands a note to CROMWELL, *saying,*
  "From General IRETON, my Lord;" *then retires.*

    CROMWELL *alone, takes the note and reads.*

The Parliament are met—my goodlie, Godly
Parliament—no, no, not mine, but Barebones'.
What a name! They would o'erturn all known forms
Of law and government, would I but let them.
I have failed indeed in this. They are worse
Than were the Danes or Normans. Those fellows,
Preaches, Feakes, and Powell, preach that Cromwell
Is the Man of Sin—the Old Dragon and the Beast
Foretold in the Revelation. I've had enough
Of this fooling. Ireton! Ireton, I say!—
There's terror in his looks and name—
    IRETON *enters.*] My son, go to the House,
Forthwith—bid the members repair to Whitehall,
And give back their authority into the hands
Of him from whom they had received it.
If these reformers, who are some thirty—
I know them all—ask for a warrant, call in
A company of soldiers; take my own guard,
If needs be; clear the House, and hither bring
The keys. It must be done—this the best way
To do it.

IRETON.

And shall be.

CROMWELL.

He likes this service.
What a stout heart that is! My Oliver's was even such,
But Richard's is a gewgaw for fair dames.

CAREW *enters.*

General, the Military Council have decided
That, finding Parliaments such unstable
And unwieldy things, that you be solemnly
Installed the Lord Protector of the Commonwealth
Of England, Scotland, and Ireland, and do await
Your presence in Westminster Hall. They beg
You'll pardon this lack of ceremony,
But the State requires it.

CROMWELL.

Thanks, my good friend;
I will attend, though I would rather not assume
Fresh cares.   [*Exit* CAREW.

IRETON *enters with Speaker, bringing keys.*

CROMWELL.

Ha! Gentlemen; welcome, Gentlemen;
  With a smile.]
My son, you did escort them in due form.

SPEAKER.

We would resign the power you conferred on us,
Unworthy instruments, unequal to the task,
And pray for your dismission.

CROMWELL.

Nay, my good friend,
Why so? How is this? You have scarcely entered

Upon our service; but if it needs must be,
Why, it must be. I have appealed to God
Before you already. I know it is a tender thing
To make appeals to God. Then fare ye well.
[*Speaker exit one side;* CROMWELL *and* IRETON *the other.*

SCENE FIFTH.

Westminster Hall.

A Chair of State, with a rich carpet and cushions.—A Commissioner of the Great Seal at each hand.—The Judges on both sides.—The Lord Mayor and Aldermen on the right, and the members of the Council on the left.—Triumphal Music.—CROMWELL enters with a splendid retinue.

CROMWELL.

My loving, honorable, and much honored friends,
Why would ye summon me, an humble citizen,
To leave the calm and equal walks of privacy,
For the toilsome and uneasy race of greatness?
I thank ye for the honors ye would confer;
But pray ye to confer them on one worthier.

INGOLDSBY.

Cromwell's the name, the worthiest England
Ever bore, to wear the honors that her people give.

LISLE.

Here is the institute of Government,
Duly sealed, and here am I to administer
The oath gives unto England's sole and only use
Her worthiest son, as Protector of the Realm.

CROMWELL, *raising his hand.*

Since such is your and the people's gracious will,
Here do I swear, in all humility,

Her honor to preserve by land and sea,
From pole to pole.

The Lords Commissioners deliver up to CROMWELL *the*
Purse and Seals.

LORDS COMMISSIONERS.

The purse and seals, your Highness;
Pointing to the Chair of State.] And that your seat.

LORD MAYOR OF LONDON.

This too, with London's love and loyalty, my sword.

CROMWELL.

Nay, Sir, as Cromwell's friend, keep this.
In greatest stress the Londoners e'er proved true;
So may I find them ever.
      Advances.]
Protector of the Realm—in all things King, save name!
The wide world envies me—the air is rent
With praises of my deeds—each act a virtue,
And many great acts mine that never yet
I dreamed of. So runs the world; a few short years
Protector of the Realm, a few short minutes
May be your span of life. But for this mail,
                              [*Strikes his breast.*
Some secret foe had long ere this probed
My heart's mysteries, and unveiled to earth
What Heaven only knows; for all my deeds,
Ay, even my motives, yet shall be unfolded
To the world, though it may be not until
Long hereafter; but probed they will be.
Regicide one age, the next I shall be lauded
To the skies as Godlike, Freedom's Father!
Strange destiny is mine—an humble wanderer
In a savage clime, I thought to be,
      5*

When he, whose head paid forfeit for the act,
Compelled my sojourn here, and made me
More than King; for I've o'erleaped all wonted forms,
And out of the line direct, though of royal blood,
I reign entire master of the Realm—
Its meanest and its mightiest, officers to my will.

ATTENDANT, *advancing.*

Ambassador of France, my Lord.

CROMWELL.

      Give him admittance.

AMBASSADOR.

France sends her greeting unto the Lord Protector,
And woos his friendship and his favor.

CROMWELL.

We thank His Majesty, and trust the love
Our people and ourselves now entertain
For him may be preserved. Say this is
From Cromwell unto Mazarin. Prithee,
Your presence at our feast to-day.
 Presenting him to Ladies.] Our Lady Cromwell,
And our friends, fair Sir.
 Officer hands a paper.] From Spain an Ambassador
Attends. France *and* Spain—France *or* Spain—
Now come the troubles of our greatness.
Portugal too doth wait; and from the Netherlands
There is an embassy; the United Provinces
Now sue for peace, on terms most favorable
To us—which we will grant, for our great Blake
Has swept the seas even of Von Tromp
And his masthead broom. The triumphs of our flag
Shed a glory on our rule unequalled

By the past—if Cromwell lives, never to be equalled
In the *great hereafter.*

.

I'll have no foreign wars, our foes subdued
Or peace insured; for there are troublous tongues
Enough at home.   Though scarce established
As their Lord Protector, idle, venomous spirits
Do menace me—even the Preachers dare denounce me.
The system I in Ireland adopted, speedily worked
My ends; I'll try it here.   Ireton, I have heard
That our late friend, Harrison, wags his tongue
Against us.   He was a master spirit in our cause;
May prove such against us.   The Tower
Were the safest place for him.   There's likewise
A stubborn, wrongheaded schoolmaster called Vowell,
Who has been most treasonable in his course;
He is not of much note, and has few friends
To feel revenge—let him be hanged—
'Twill give their idle brains somewhat to muse
Upon; and that young fellow, Gerald,
I've seen the boy, a murderer by his looks—
Let him swing for it—be instant—
No paltering now.   [*Exit* IRETON.
            Faith, I would rather have taken
A shepherd's staff than this Protectorship.
My Genius hates this show of greatness.
New England should have been my home;
No shadows would have crossed my pure intents.
There the untutored savage I might have moulded
In the true ways of life; in nature and association
They're prepared.   Here, every tree
And stone, ay, every star tells men of Princes
And their pageantry.   The history of all times
Teaches of despots and despotic rule.

Though for some short-lived season men may have tried
Self-government, 'twas e'er to fall under an iron hand,
That crushed them into obedience.   ·
                        I have been swept along
By the swift current of fierce events, and find
Myself upon a throne—a throne of cares and fears—
My myrmidons, jealousy, hate, deceit,
And all the fellest passions of the human heart.
Men do not love me—why, they cannot say,
Save that I have o'ertopped them.   [*Enter* INGOLDSBY.
                        Ha! Ingoldsby—
What news?

INGOLDSBY.

        Great discontent among
Our quondam friends.

CROMWELL.

        Why so?   Have I not told them
I would not be lord over them; but one that is resolved
To be a fellow-servant, to the intent
Of this great affair?

INGOLDSBY.

True, true; but now the House debated, whether
They should consent to have the Government
Vested in a single person and a Parliament,
And carried it but by five voices.
   Enter IRETON.]

CROMWELL.

              Indeed! what more?

IRETON.

One said, that as God had made him
Instrumental in cutting down tyranny
In one individual, so could he not endure

To see the liberties of the nation shackled
By another, whose right to the Government
Could not be measured otherwise than by the length
Of his sword, which alone had emboldened him
To command his commanders.

CROMWELL.

And yet they thrust it on me.
What more was said?

INGOLDSBY.

Another as the Prophet
Unto Ahab said—"Hast thou killed and also
Taken possession?"

CROMWELL.

Such words of me! I had not dreamed
They thought it. Killed, did they say? You know
I did not do it; it was ordained by them;
My signature wrung from a father's bleeding heart,
At sight of his eldest son a corpse transfixed.
If this is my reward
For years of toil—for fondest hopes crushed
At their consummation—for Heaven's own ways
(Mine were then most pure), all set aside,
And worldly courses taken—hereafter
I will be ruler of myself and of this realm—
Preserve my life, though at the cost of myriads.
I have made England great, greater than e'er before,
And I will rule. Ingoldsby, let them say on,
Ay, gibe like monkeys—I tell you, Sir,
The time will come when they will offer me
The crown. Go you, and order three regiments
To march into the city; seize the most noisy
Of these brawlers; place a guard at the door
Of the House, and lay this recognition

On a table in the lobby, for their signature.
I have foreseen all this, and now *will know*
My friends.   This binds them neither to propose
Or consent to alter the Government
As it is now settled in a single person
And Parliament.   I will have my spies
In every regiment, in almost every house,
And in the very bed-chamber of this Charles II.,
As they clepe him—at Cologne and at Paris.
I have done with peace and rest—there is
No rest for me but in the grave—the grave.

This kingdom I will divide into military governments,
To arrest, imprison, and bind over
All dangerous and suspected persons,
Without the power of appeal to any
But the Protector himself and his Council;
And all who have borne arms for the King,
Or were of the royal party, shall be
Decimated.   There will no longer be a cant
Of liberty.   They are not fit for it,
Who fatten on distrust, and, gorged,
Would fill the realm with it.   There now are
In the ports a hundred ships of various sizes;—
Penn and Venables shall hasten to the settlements
Of Spain and seize on them;
Thence to James River, and reduce to allegiance
Unto me, those colonies which dare adhere
To Charles, cleping themselves the "Old Dominion;"
I'll give them a new rule, whose seeds shall yet
O'ertop the world;—while Blake shall add
To his well-won honors, and seize Spain's treasure-ships.
France must be our friend, even though Spain
Is our foe; yet now proposes I should be seated

On the throne.   Ireton, go you and give my order
That Penruddock and Groves be beheaded at Exeter;
Jones and his friends be hanged; the residue
Who were concerned in the rising at Salisbury,
Be sent to Barbadoes and sold as slaves!
Issue my declaration, prohibiting
All sequestered clergymen of the Church
Of England from preaching or using the Liturgy,
As ministers, either in public or private;
And command all Roman Catholic priests
To quit the kingdom under pain of death.
Forbid the publication in print of any news
Whatever, without permission from the Secretary of State.
There are three argosies in port, taken by Blake;
See that Friend Fox be recompensed—this done,
The residue retain for England's honor.
Thus Cromwell seeks redress.
Send instantly an embassy to the Duke of Savoy,
To intercede in behalf of the persecuted Vaudois.
Our brother of France unites in this—we will it so.
Then let him haste to Rome, with our command
That all persecutions of God's elect shall cease,
Or Cromwell's cannon's roar shall echo
Through St. Angelo.   [*Exeunt.*

Enter COLONEL JEPHSON, ASHE, *and* SIR CHARLES PACK.

COLONEL JEPHSON.

My friends, what may we do to stay
These plots against our General and ourselves,
Which rise on every hand at every hour?

ASHE.

Make him our King!—beseech him that he will be pleased
To take upon himself the Government

According to the ancient Constitution—
Then will their hopes and plots be at an end.

SIR CHARLES PACK.

This was my thought; and here have I prepared
An humble address and remonstrance
Of the knights, citizens, and burgesses now assembled
In the Parliament of the Commonwealth,
Praying he will accept this power.
The title I have left blank—shall we present it?

JEPHSON.

Ay, and fill the blank with KING. We'll find him
In the Tapestrie Chamber. Come, we'll present it
On the instant.   [*Exeunt.*

SCENE SIXTH.

Whitehall.

Enter CROMWELL, LAMBERT, FLEETWOOD, *and* DESBOR-
OUGH.

CROMWELL.

Oh, what a troublous thing is greatness!
I once knew peace—sweet peace of mind—but it is fled
Forever. There is no safety now for me
From dastard cut-throats, save an armed guard,
And all the attendants make kings slaves.
Free in my nature, I would have been free,
Free as the wild deer roves New England's woods.
He stayed me in my course of usefulness,
And made me what I am now, what I am yet
To be. Fleetwood my son, my brother Desborough,
And my friend Lambert—*they* would have me king,
These lawyers and civilians—what think ye

Of this name ?   The power I have is greater
Than any king's for ages past.

DESBOROUGH.

Nay, Cromwell, entertain it not ;
There is more matter than you perceive in this ;
Those who would put this on you, sure, are no enemies
To Charles Stuart.

FLEETWOOD.

Methinks it would draw ruin on yourself
And friends.   General, eschew this act.

CROMWELL.

Oh, ye are a couple of precise, scrupulous fellows.
Lambert, what say you ?

LAMBERT.

                    As do these friends, your kinsmen,—
Touch not the diadem.

CROMWELL.

Well, well, I would do naught without consent
Of the army.   Hasten to the House, and put them off
From doing any thing further in this matter.
But lo, whom have we here ?

Enter SPEAKER *and others.*

SPEAKER.

My Lord, herewith do I present to you
The humble petition and advice of the Parliament,
Setting forth the advantages of regal government,
And the nation's confidence in a new Sovereign—
Yourself their choice.

CROMWELL.

My gentle friends, I thank you, but must decline.

SPEAKER, *presenting the diadem.*

Here is the diadem.

CROMWELL.

What! would ye tempt me
With this golden bawble, which at the best
Is but a feather in a man's cap?   I should not be
An honest man, did I not tell you that I
Cannot accept of the government, nor undertake
The trouble and charge of it.   I, who have tried it
More than any one—indeed, I cannot undertake
The government with the title of King.
This receive, I pray you, as my answer
To this great and weighty business.*

SPEAKER.

This must we to the Parliament relate,
Who'll much regret refusal to their will.

CROMWELL.

Give them my thanks;—as Lord Protector
I will rule the realm as God directs me.
'Tis a weighty trust; I pray ye lighten it
As best ye may, by your collected wisdom,
Unto which I'll bow, so long as England's welfare
Is your aim.   My thanks to one and all;
My friends, at even I will meet ye.   [*Exeunt.*
The diadem of England mine!   Her fleets,
Her fortresses, her coffers, armies, all are mine!
All save her people's love—that which I most
Had prized—and yet they'd have me take
The name of King—that bane of greatness.
I sought it not, and ne'er will own it.   I have made
England great, Scotland and Ireland too,
And won a name which shall be mine alone

* Cromwell's words.

For every age throughout the world. I made
My people free—redressed their wrongs, and placed
The power in their own hands—but ah, alas!
I found them ill prepared for self-government;
They are so trammelled by old ties and customs.
Whitehall and Westminster, St. James, the Tower,
All speak of regal rule; old laws and usages
Are seared upon their hearts; they cannot walk
In the new paths I've marked; paths must be laid out
In a new land, where there is naught but freedom
To be seen. There in New England I might have fixed
The People's Rule—a rule that shall o'ermaster
Every other form, and last till the last trump
Shall sound, *if men but unto themselves be true.*
Ah! that dread tertian ague seizes now!
Why comes this sickness on me at this hour?
Thou bleeding form, thou canst not say I plucked
Thy diadem to perch it on my brow. Years
Now have numbered their troublous minutes o'er,
And yet thou visitest me, thou murdered King.
I will descend unto your charnel-house,
And gaze upon your slumbers—peaceful slumbers.
Shall such be mine?   [*Takes a light.*
   IRETON *enters.*]   Ha! Ireton! what now?
Thy brow doth lower portentous as the thunder-cloud.

IRETON.

An old and faithful soldier of your guard
Craves instantly the Lord Protector's ear.

CROMWELL.

Give him admittance. He should have said
His General's. I hate these titles from my long-tried
      friends.

Soldier enters.]   Ha! what wouldst thou, my brave
fellow?

SOLDIER.

Full credence to my tale, and instant action,
To cut short a deed too dreadful to be thought on.

CROMWELL.

What deed? Speak! speak!—how every tale unmans
me!

SOLDIER.

One Dr. Hewett, Sir Henry Slugsby, and he
Who was brave Colonel Sexby, with him
Who is called Snydercombe, gave me this purse
And these bright jewels, in order to procure
Admittance to the chapel at Whitehall.

CROMWELL.

They are my friends. You did accept and gave it them.
Was it well done? I saved your life at peril
Of mine own at Drogheda, striking aside
The pike was at your throat—and you'd risk mine
For a paltry bribe!

SOLDIER.

Ay, those wild Irish—

CROMWELL.

Nay, nay, not so;—they are a gallant and a misused race.
See their condition now under just laws;
Their land is teeming with productiveness.
This I, Cromwell, did. But for your story.

SOLDIER.

Into the chapel they have but now borne
Combustibles, and placed a match to secure

The conflagration of the palace before midnight,
While they, with arms prepared, shall shut you up
Within the flames.

CROMWELL.

Oh! horrible, most horrible.   Ireton,
Take this ring.   Seize them at once; let instant death
Be theirs, if that his tale prove true.

IRETON.

I have them, one and all.   Fleetwood and Desborough
Now await your will.   [*Exit.*

CROMWELL.

My gallant guard, take this—a trifling gift.
Your self-approval be your best reward.
But for myself, I'll make you captain in my guard,
With treble pay.   Attend on General Ireton
In this melancholy task.   [*Exit soldier.*
Who would be great, if blood must be its price?
Or I must let these bloodhounds tear me
Limb from limb, or wade myself in blood.
Charles, Charles, thou art avenged!   Could I,
I would not wake you into life.
                              I almost wish
To lay me by thy side.   I will once more
Look on thee in thy rest.
              [*Takes the light, and retires slowly.*

SCENE SEVENTH.

Vault—King Charles's Tomb.

ELIZABETH CROMWELL *enters, dressed in white, with flowers, and, singing, strews them round, and lays them on the tomb.*

Thou sleepest in peace, thou murdered innocence!
I told my Charles I would do this.   Nightly I've decked
His couch with flowers most fair, year after year.
Alas! poor king—father to my heart's Lord.
This tender office ere long, I feel, must fall
To other hands.   Sleep ou—sleep on—sleep on!
A step—who comes?   It is my father—what does he here?
I must be gone.

　　[ELIZABETH *flits round to one side, then across the back,*
　　and escapes.

CROMWELL *enters.*

I heard a voice—methought a seraph's voice,
And perfumed air did greet me as I came.
Do angels watch his bier?   What! flowers
Blooming all about his marble couch—the tenderest
Springing from it.   He sleeps in peace,
Or sure these sweet attendants all would fail
And fade away—*they* are the ministering spirits
Of the blest.   If such *his* happy end,
Why may I not look for a release
From all life's cares and toils?
Was his hand bloodless?
Mine's incarnadined!   They who sought his fall,
And now seek mine—these demi-devils—.
That they might gain their ends, sure forged the tale
That my son's death was planned and urged

By him, that they might damn my soul.
King, kinsman, royal master, rouse from thy slumbers,
And smile on me forgiveness!   Think of the agony
A father feels, his butchered son before him.

   Opens the lid of tomb.]

What! can it be that envious time has leashed
Its ravenous worms, that thus thou lookest
As when thou livedst, and on thy face that smile
Thou worest, uttering thy last "Remember!"
Men doubt thy meaning—alas! I read it well;
For ne'er have I forgotten thee.   By day, by night,
At feast, at fast—waking or dreaming, in court
Or camp, in peaceful council or dread carnage—
There, before me, ever rose thy august head,
And, bleeding, lisped "Remember."   [*A shriek.*
Hark, that piercing shriek!—that seraph's voice—my
   child's—
It is my child's.   She comes—what would she here?

   ELIZABETH *enters wildly.*

Blood, blood, blood—nothing but blood!
My dearest brother's, my most honored king's;
And now my reverend, reverenced friend's
Must swell the turgid stream.   Who are you
Have usurped my place, and keep your vigils
By this sainted form?   Hence, hence, hence!
This is my fond prerogative, given me
By my loving lord, that should have been—
The king that yet shall be.   Come, come, I pray thee,
Come!   I know thee not; and yet, there is a majesty
In thy mien betokens power and compels my reverence.
Come, come; *thou* yet mayst save him.   Come, this way,
This way.   [*She, retiring, beckons to him.*

CROMWELL, *following.*

Oh! woful sight.   It hath o'erpowered me.

Scene changes to banqueting hall.   ELIZABETH *enters, beck-
      oning to* CROMWELL, *who follows.*

My child, my child, what means this frenzy?
Whither, say, whither wouldst thou lead me?
What, what wouldst thou?

ELIZABETH, *looking wildly.*

Blood, blood!   No, no, not blood; that thou canst give
      me.
But life, dear life—the life, once taken, gone
Forever, never, never to be returned.
      Awakening to consciousness.]
Father! is't thou, my father? my fond, my doting father?
My mind has wandered; but I know you now.
The child of thy tender love kneels for a boon—
The boon of an old man's life—a life worth
But a few brief years at best.   Thou knowest
What 'tis to die.   I saw you there—I know 'twas you—
Where death sweet office long hath given me.

CROMWELL.

Ah me! ah me!   How all my honors shrink
To nothingness, my glories fade from sight,
And memory pictures horrors to my view!
What is it thou askest, my fair, though faded child?

ELIZABETH.

Ah! now thou art my father.   Tender tones,
Long, long unheard, though never yet forgotten,
Are ushered in by smiles—my father's smiles,
The smiles were sweetest to my infant heart,
Though, to my woman's, strangers.   Why wert thou

Ever great? Was to be goodness not enough for you?
Give me his life—my friend's—old Dr. Hewett's.
He has been guilty of no crime, I know.

CROMWELL.

Crime! thou sweet innocent. *Thy* life was doomed.
Was there no crime in that? Thy mother's, sister's,
Brothers', father's—all! He would have made
Whitehall—one hecatomb.

ELIZABETH.

Oh, horrible! Art sure? I thought that he loved me.
I loved him ever.

CROMWELL.

                    Most sure. Thy uncle, Desborough—
Thy brothers, Fleetwood, Ingoldsby, and Ireton,
Took him and others in the very act,
                              And now they die—
Thunder heard.]
Hark! how the elements are rent at bare recital
Of their dread intent! The lightning quivers
Through these vaulted domes, and horrid echoes
Chase from room to room.

ELIZABETH.

Their shrieks! their dying shrieks! Ah me! ah me!
Father, I have borne much—could have borne more;
But this *his* treachery takes such horrid form,
I shrink at thought of it. My heart!
My Charles! my brain!

LADY CROMWELL, LADY LAMBERT, INGOLDSBY, *enter as she
is swooning in* CROMWELL's *arms.*

LADY CROMWELL.

My child! my child!   [*They place her on a couch.*
6

CROMWELL, *sinking down by the couch.*

My child! my child! Support her, Heaven,
And preserve her senses.

          Ha! Ingoldsby, what news?
Thunder heard again.]

INGOLDSBY.

      The elements are racked;
Disjoined, our loftiest buildings topple to the dust;
St. Paul's spire, reeling, groans. The rooks
And daws make black the air, and even
The tiny martlet quails the heart
With its shrill cries, driven from its ancestral
Moss-grown home.

CROMWELL.

What day is this, that man and nature,
Thus conjoined, do rack earth to its foundations?

LADY CROMWELL.

My lord, it is your day, your own auspicious day—
THE THIRD DAY OF SEPTEMBER!

CROMWELL.

Ah! is it so?   [*Turning to* DOCTOR.
    How does my child?

ELIZABETH *murmuring low words.*]

DOCTOR.

The wild delirium feasts upon her brain,
And burns up every sense, save some dark,
Dread memories. She raves of Charles—of blood.

CROMWELL.

My dearest daughter and fair nature—both
Whom I've best loved and worshipped, next to God—

Both crazed and mad!
    Ah! my old sickness comes upon me.
   "O Lord! thy miserable servant
Bows to thy will in all humility,
And craves thy grace.   Bless thou this people.
Thou hast made me a mean instrument
To do them some good, and Thee, I trust,
Some service.   Many there are have set
Too high a value on me, though others wish,
And would be glad of, my decease.
However thou dost dispose of me, my Lord,
Continue to do good to and abide
With them.   Give them consistency of judgment—
One heart and mutual love, to go on
With the work of reformation, and make
The name of *Christ*, a name at which every knee
Shall bend and every head shall bow,
Glorious throughout the world.   Teach those
Who look too much upon thy instruments,
To more upon *Thyself* depend.   Pardon all those
(They are thy people) would trample upon the dust
Of this poor worm, for our blessed Redeemer's sake."*

  Ireton *enters, taking his hand.*]
      How now, my Ireton,
How is my child?

       IRETON.
    She is dead!

   CROMWELL, *caressing* ELIZABETH.
Dead! nay, nay.
    Gone! gone! gone home!
       I too shall go.
Her sainted spirit heralds mine.
    * Guizot.

My friends—
Let Richard be my heir.   Guard ye him well.
At my interment, *I pray you*, have no vain ceremonials.
'Tis but the form that dies.
Publish to the world that Cromwell's last words
Were, that
            " Where the Spirit of the Lord is,
There is Liberty,"   .
                And that 'tis cradled
In New England now, to grow a Hercules
Shall bestride all earth.
So Cromwell's teachings yet shall rule the world.
Mankind shall say, in times to come, that here died
" The best thing ever England did."*

A fearful peal of thunder and flash of lightning. IRETON
                struck dead.

Hark to that fearful peal,
                    As though heaven crashed
    Seeing IRETON.]
Thy knell, my Ireton.
                Thus only couldst *thou* die.

A brilliant light from above thrown upon CROMWELL, *kneeling by* ELIZABETH. *His head drops on her form.*

The Gates of Glory open stand,
                And I am summoned.†

                TABLEAU.

            Curtain falls slowly.

* Carlyle.
† The Court of France went into mourning, wearing dark-blue velvet.
—*Guizot.*

WS - #0085 - 261023 - C0 - 229/152/7 - PB - 9781330901670 - Gloss Lamination